Trust
the
Whisper

Also by Kathy Izard

For Adults

The Hundred Story Home:
A Memoir about Finding Faith in Ourselves and Something Bigger

The Last Ordinary Hour:
Living Life Now That Nothing Will Ever Be the Same

For Children

A Good Night for Mr. Coleman

Grace Heard a Whisper

Trust *the* *Whisper*

HOW ANSWERING QUIET CALLINGS INSPIRES
EXTRAORDINARY STORIES OF ORDINARY GRACE

KATHY IZARD

BakerBooks
a division of Baker Publishing Group
Grand Rapids, Michigan

© 2024 by Kathy Izard

Published by Baker Books
a division of Baker Publishing Group
Grand Rapids, Michigan
BakerBooks.com

Printed in the United States of America

Library of Congress Cataloging-in-Publication Data
Names: Izard, Kathy, 1963– author.
Title: Trust the whisper : how answering quiet callings inspires extraordinary stories of ordinary grace / Kathy Izard.
Description: Grand Rapids, Michigan : Baker Books, a division of Baker Publishing Group, [2024] | Includes bibliographical references.
Identifiers: LCCN 2023043652 | ISBN 9781540904140 (paper) | ISBN 9781540904195 (casebound) | ISBN 9781493445752 (ebook)
Subjects: LCSH: Inspiration—Religious aspects—Christianity. | God (Christianity)—Omnipresence. | Grace (Theology).
Classification: LCC BV4501.3 .I994 2024 | DDC 231.7—dc23/eng/20231213
LC record available at https://lccn.loc.gov/2023043652

Some names and details have been changed to protect the privacy of the individuals involved.

The author is represented by the literary agency of The Blythe Daniel Agency, Inc.

Cover design by Studio Gearbox, Chris Gilbert.

Emojis are from the open-source library OpenMoji (https://openmoji.org/) under the Creative Commons license CC BY-SA 4.0 (https://creativecommons.org/licenses/by-sa/4.0/legalcode).

24 25 26 27 28 29 30   7 6 5 4 3 2 1

For Lauren, Kailey, Emma, and Maddie

May you always trust your whispers
to lead you back to who
you were always meant to be.

Contents

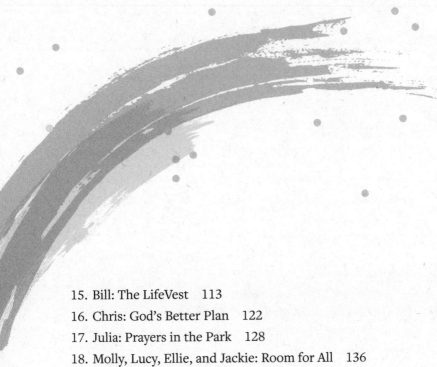

Author's Note

This collection of stories is how I began to understand God.

If you already believe in God,
I hope this book strengthens your faith.

If you have been questioning God,
I hope this book helps you find faith
in yourself and something bigger.

I am certain only that God is whispering to each of us,
not what God might be whispering to you.

1

Denver: The First Whisper

It begins with a whisper.

That little voice inside you telling you to *do* something that feels inconvenient, unexpected, and uncomfortable.

It might start with something small, like encouraging you to speak to a complete stranger, or something big, like urging you to accept a job for which you feel unqualified. It might even be insisting you attempt something that feels highly unlikely you could ever achieve, like writing a book when you have never written anything longer than an email.

I am willing to bet that no matter your age, you have already heard at least one whisper in your life, but you might have dismissed it as simply a wild hope or an unrealistic dream.

The kind of whisper I'm talking about is one that is difficult to ignore. It rises from inside your soul and slips not only into your dreams but into your every waking hour. It stubbornly persists, quietly demanding your attention. This kind of true soul whisper eventually becomes so insistent you have to decide: Do you spend the rest of your life listening to it, or keep pretending you never heard it?

The first time I can remember hearing such an insistent whisper, I was a happily married, forty-four-year-old mom with four daughters. I owned my own graphic design business and regularly volunteered at our daughters' schools, our church, and in the community. My life was good—really, it was more than good. So why did I have an underlying restless feeling that there was something else I was supposed to be doing with my life? I had this constant sense that the life I was living was not what I was meant to be doing. But at the same time, I had no idea what else I should do or how to begin looking.

My life plans had typically been driven by the two loudest voices in my head: my "to-do voice" and my "fear voice." My to-do voice kept me focused on daily tasks, which included all the rational reminders like *pay the mortgage, feed the dog*, and *meet the deadline*. Even though those things kept me busy, I secretly had other ideas for my life that included wanting to do something that truly mattered. Designing logos and creating brochures was not the type of meaningful work I had envisioned for myself growing up. I even had a folder in my office labeled "Change the World," where I kept magazine and newspaper clippings of people whom I thought were making a difference in ways both big and small. When I thought about making a change in my own life, I considered going to graduate school. But how would I do that with four kids? And besides, I had no idea what I would even study.

On days when I was particularly frustrated with my present career, I would reread articles about inspirational people, hoping to unlock the door to my own potential. But whenever I imagined how I might change the world and leave it a better place, my fear voice would interrupt my dreams to discourage any new life plan, listing all the reasons it would be impossible. That voice would drown out any new dream by reminding me of all the ways I might fail and convincing me that I was only qualified to be what I currently was: a graphic designer.

For years, my to-do voice and my fear voice combined to keep me stuck on my very safe and logical life plan: building a good family, running a successful business, and giving back in some small ways. I was so busy with career climbing, bill paying, and child raising, I didn't think it really mattered what my soul had to say about it. It wasn't until I began watching my teenage daughters chase their dreams that I recognized how fully I had forgotten my own.

The nagging feeling that I had another purpose never left me, but I could not understand how to find a new direction. In retrospect, I know that is because I was looking for a great big sign with flashing lights to point me in the right direction, announcing, "This is your life purpose! Turn right here!" Maybe I believed that when I found such an obvious sign, then my to-do voice would take over and my fear voice wouldn't object.

But, of course, there was never a neon sign. There was only this gentle nudge urging me to seek something else even though everything in my life was *fine*. Just fine. Eventually, I found what I was looking for in a much quieter way than I expected. And it began with a whisper.

· · · ·

For over ten years, I volunteered with my family once a month in a Charlotte, North Carolina, soup kitchen that was part of the Roof Above homeless service agency (formerly called the Urban Ministry Center). We liked helping in the soup kitchen because my husband, Charlie, and I wanted to teach our four daughters the value of giving back while at the same time understanding how much we receive by serving others. To be honest, however, our Sunday soup kitchen shift was also a great way to feel good about not going to church that day. When our girls were young, it was a constant battle to wrestle them into tights, dresses, and shiny shoes so they would look presentable in the pew. There was no dress code in the soup kitchen, so serving here on Sundays only required jeans and a smile.

15

On soup kitchen Sunday, our family would arrive at 8:30 a.m. to help make over six hundred ham sandwiches and thirty gallons of vegetable soup. During our monthly five-hour shift, we would serve lunch to those experiencing homelessness and help with the laundry and mail services. Even though I was restlessly seeking a purpose in my life, I never thought what I was looking for could be found at the soup kitchen. I believed homelessness was an unsolvable problem. What could a graphic designer and mom do about such a complex issue?

All that changed in 2007, when I had an encounter that felt like a divine appointment with a man named Denver Moore. While Denver had been homeless for over thirty years in Texas, he ended up cowriting a *New York Times* bestseller titled *Same Kind of Different as Me*. My mom suggested I read the book because she thought its stories about homelessness would resonate with my own volunteer experience—and they did. Denver told heartbreaking tales about his years on the streets, as well as how he met his cowriter Ron Hall and Debbie, Ron's wife, who helped at a Fort Worth soup kitchen. The couple formed a deep friendship with Denver, and his impact on their lives was transformative. Eventually, Debbie asked Denver to live with them, and in doing so, she ended one man's homelessness.

This was the part of the story I never expected—the idea of actually *ending* someone's homelessness. After reading the book, I could not shake the shame I felt that in all my years of volunteering at our soup kitchen, I had never befriended anyone, much less invited them to live with us. For so many years, I had stayed safely behind the stainless steel lunch counter, serving people with a smile because I was afraid of being asked to do anything more.

After reading Denver's book, however, I began to hear my first insistent whisper. It wasn't about getting to know someone at the soup kitchen or inviting them to live with me. It was about the authors of the book.

The whisper I kept hearing was, *Invite them to speak.*

It made no sense.

From reading the book, I knew Debbie had died of cancer but Ron and Denver were both very much alive. Why would I invite them to speak? Our soup kitchen was not planning an event like a fundraiser where speakers would be needed, and even if it was, I had no expertise in planning or organizing events. It was inconvenient, unexpected, and uncomfortable to imagine listening to that whisper.

Yet every time I saw the golden-yellow book cover on my bedside table, I heard the same unmistakable whisper.

Invite them to speak.

The whisper became so persistent, I had two choices: listen or pretend I never heard it.

So, I finally listened.

Six months later, Ron and Denver arrived in Charlotte for the fundraiser I was chairing with the help of a dozen friends. We called the event "True Blessings," and it became more popular than we could have imagined. More than one thousand people registered to attend our luncheon in a hotel ballroom. For weeks, I had been both excited and terrified, wondering why I had listened to that whisper and worrying about how it was all going to turn out. I now know the reason was so that I could have a moment with Denver that would change my life forever.

As part of their two-day visit, I took Denver on a tour of our soup kitchen. When I picked him up at the hotel, he was wearing his signature outfit: black shirt, black tie, black suit, and black fedora. He appeared dressed to impress, and I was excited to witness how the famous author would inspire some of our homeless neighbors.

As I led him on the tour, however, Denver was not speaking. I showed him our art, street soccer, and garden programs, which were designed not to make happier homeless people but as ways to connect and build relationships. First-time visitors were usually impressed with these programs, yet Denver listened without commenting. Following me throughout the campus, he didn't say a word or ask a single question. He seemed to be growing increasingly impatient, though, as if the more I spoke the less he thought I had to say. In truth, Denver was just waiting for me to show him what he considered the single most important feature of a homeless service agency—one that I was about to understand we didn't have.

After a twenty-minute tour filled with awkward silence, I realized that I had not managed to amaze the famous author with our good works, but I still did not understand why. Feeling frustrated, I turned to lead us out the main door, and that is when Denver finally decided to speak. We were standing in the main building by the reception desk, with a staircase to our right. All around us were dozens of people hurrying to get mail or a meal, so I could barely hear Denver when he asked, "Can we go upstairs now?"

I wasn't sure what he meant. I had already showed him everything worth seeing. Why did he want to go upstairs?

"There is nothing up there, just offices," I told him.

"Where are the beds?" Denver asked.

"The beds?" I echoed.

Had he not been listening on my tour? We were a day ministry, not a shelter. Surely, after thirty years on the streets, Denver understood the differences between different homeless service agencies. But he let me know he'd been listening to every word I had said.

"You mean to tell me you do all this good in the day, and you lock 'em out to the bad at night?" Denver asked.

Was that what I was saying? For ten years, I had been volunteering there. For ten years, I knew we opened our gates at 8:30 a.m. and closed them at 4:30 p.m. And for ten years, I had never once asked myself what happened outside of that time.

"Does that make any sense to you?" Denver asked.

Of course it didn't. Once he said it that way, I couldn't think about it any other way.

"Are *you* going to do something about it?" Denver asked.

That was the question that changed everything for me.

Are you going to do something about it?

Denver had shown me the problem in a way I could never unsee. I could never go back to serving soup without thinking about "the bad at night." I could never again watch those gates closing in the afternoon or opening in the morning and pretend not to know that there was an excruciating stretch in between during which we were providing no help whatsoever.

Just like that first whisper, *Invite them to speak*, a second whisper began. This time, I kept hearing Denver's question: *Are you going to do something about it?*

Again, the whisper felt inconvenient, unexpected, and uncomfortable. My fear voice hissed at me—in case I was unaware—that I was completely unqualified to do anything about the homeless problem in Charlotte. My to-do voice steadily reminded me that I already had a life plan with a business and clients, and this idea was in no way part of anything I had outlined.

This new whisper did not care about that, and it would not give in. It was insistent.

The soft sound from my soul persisted in pushing me to imagine that I could *Do something about it* even though I had no idea what that might be. The whisper became like that neon sign I had been looking for telling me where to turn. I worried that listening might mean making a huge mistake by veering off my carefully constructed life plan. It turned out, however, that listening would not be a detour but rather my destiny.

After two months of wrestling with my new whisper, I closed my graphic design business to accept a job working for Roof Above, not in the soup kitchen but to help develop a housing program. I immersed myself in the homeless service world and began to figure out what doing something about it even meant.[1]

• • • •

Since that meeting in 2007, everything in my life has changed, from how I spend my time to what I think is important. My professional title has shifted from graphic designer to program director to development director, and finally to author.

As each whisper came along, I began gaining confidence every time I made a detour, despite not understanding the destination. I became willing to divert from my *life plan* and follow a *life path*. It has become clear to me those whispers are what I should've been listening to all along, instead of only trusting my to-do voice and my fear voice.

It was another whisper that urged me to *Write it down*. The nudge made no sense at the time; I hadn't written anything since college. But I began trusting each whisper, which led to publishing four books, including the one you are reading.

To be clear, none of this was my plan. Each of these new chapters has been the result of following some new whisper that felt inconvenient, unexpected, and uncomfortable—yet at the same time was insistent. Each whisper seemed to connect me to another piece of my own story and to help me know I was finally becoming exactly who I was meant to be.

Along the way, I've met other people who were listening to their own whispers. Hearing other people's stories has helped me understand there is a whole silent symphony I am just finally learning to hear. The people I've met and their stories of what happened when they listened to their whispers have become what I call the "God Dots" in my life. At first it was just one or two instances, which felt like extraordinary coincidences. But then some of these God Dots began connecting to each other. Someone who had been a stranger turned out to be the key to another person's story, and then, undeniably, part of a larger divine plan.

When I first noticed these God Dots, I was simply amazed by each connection, and I wondered about the likelihood of these seemingly serendipitous moments. Over time, I've come to believe that these remarkable stories are not simply coincidences.

These miraculous stories have always been happening, and the only difference is that I finally am paying attention. Through experiencing these God Dots in my own life and witnessing them in others' lives, I now believe we are surrounded by the holy all the time. Every day, extraordinary moments are unfolding. We are all connected by this grace, and our stories are woven together in astounding ways.

When you experience something that cannot be explained by coincidence or happenstance, that is your own God Dot story. When you begin to see how your small miracles interweave with others, that is connecting the God Dots. Each God Dot, each tiny story, is part of the bigger story—the one we are all here to understand. *What is this life about? What is my purpose? Is there a God? How can I be certain?*

For me, trusting the whispers in my life signaled the beginning of answering all of those questions. I'd been certain my to-do voice would guide me to discover how I would finally leave the world a better place. And although I had a lot of my own ideas, my fear voice held me back from beginning sooner. But once I stopped being so driven by my to-do voice telling me what I thought I *should* do, I could finally hear a whisper in my soul of what I was *meant* to do.

This process didn't come naturally to me, nor did I have any prescribed practice until I started trying to write it down. My in-person meeting with Denver Moore was the first time I connected a God Dot by trusting that insistent whisper to invite him to speak. After that divine encounter, I could no longer pretend I didn't hear those whispers. I had to listen.

As I kept noticing, trusting, and connecting the dots, I realized they were like the night sky. How often do we notice that there are incredible galaxies above us? Even when we do, all those stars can seem to be beautifully random until someone explains the constellations. After we are shown the celestial patterns, we can never again look up without seeing the Little Dipper and the Big

Dipper. They have always been clearly visible in the night sky; we just had to learn to recognize what we were seeing.

As you begin to read these chapters, they might at first seem to be unrelated stories, like individual and separate stars. But as you continue, you will begin to notice how one story shines into another in ways that are extraordinary. You might doubt such unlikely connections are possible. In the beginning, that is how it was for me. But what started with whispers led to noticing patterns and then to making connections, until finally the God Dots became startlingly clear to me as one incredible divine constellation.

I know there has been and will continue to be skepticism around spirituality. It is the very essence of faith to believe without evidence. But when I started paying attention, listening to those whispers and connecting the God Dots, it seemed the evidence of the holy was, and always had been, all around me.

I believe there is something each of us is meant to do in this world, whether that is mentor one child or create one work of art or help construct one building, each of which become a piece of a much bigger story. We are each like a unique thread in a divine weave, and if we do not connect our own God Dots, a hole will remain in this larger tapestry of life.

All the people in this book and their stories have helped me believe it is the small stirrings in our souls that connect us to our purpose, to each other, to God, and to our own truest story.

It begins with a whisper.

2

Frances: The Next God Dot

For years, I marveled about my meeting with Denver and how he and I came to be in the same two feet of the universe. His four questions began the ripple effect for the change in my life I had been searching for, and I was profoundly grateful for how he altered my perspective on the world. In the beginning, I thought the whisper to *Invite them to speak* was simply a lucky idea that turned out well. So when I listened to my next whisper to *Do something about it*, I tried to make myself believe I was simply making a career change, not answering some kind of quiet calling.

By the time the next unmistakable God Dot appeared in my life, I started understanding it could not be simply luck, coincidence, or even a career change. This was about faith.

After my epiphany with Denver, I became the director of a new housing program for Roof Above that we called Homeless to Homes. Even though I felt completely unqualified to accept the job, I also felt compelled to try. Dale Mullennix, executive director of the center, knew all about my meeting with Denver. As a

Baptist minister, Dale was very familiar with the idea of hearing a call in the soul to something not quite explainable. Honestly, I think Dale believed in my whisper even before I did. Maybe that is why he gave me a chance at a job that, in all likelihood, should have gone to someone more qualified.

Whether I knew what I was doing or not, we started Homeless to Homes to solve homelessness with the one thing people really needed: homes. Our program used a policy model called Housing First, which meant someone did not need to be drug-free or sober to be accepted. Just the fact that they were a human being meant they deserved housing. Like other programs successfully using this method across the country, we would offer homes to those in dire need living on the streets and move them directly into apartments. Once they were safely housed, our new tenants would then work with a case manager to address deeper needs like mental health issues or addictions.

We started with a test program, choosing thirteen people we had served for years in the soup kitchen and offering them the chance to move into a home directly from the streets. Our Homeless to Homes residents took immense pride in their new apartments and the simple pleasures of a home. Long showers. Warm baths. Cooking their own dinners. Even those with severe mental health challenges were not as difficult to serve once they had a week of sleeping in their new apartments. After thirty days, we witnessed even more remarkable outcomes. Our tenants with substance abuse issues began asking about recovery programs, and those who had dropped out of high school started pursuing GED programs. But the transformations did not change only our new tenants, they also changed us.

Before we started this program, I had never understood what a difference housing could make or believed what a transformative effect it could have. The truth is someone living on the streets, or even in a shelter, is in pure survival mode. You cannot expect someone to have conversations about their future when their current life is in chaos. The only questions that matter are how they will get their next meal or how they will survive the night. But with the safety and security of their own place to live, they can see so many more doors open with possibilities.

It was clear that our pilot program for thirteen people was not enough; we needed to do more. We dreamed of constructing our own apartment building, named Moore Place in part for the man who inspired it, Denver Moore. Moore Place would become Charlotte's first permanent supportive housing for chronically homeless men and women. Our vision was to create our own apartment community with a team of caseworkers in the building to help residents continue to improve their lives, similar to programs in other cities.

Building Moore Place would be an overwhelming task with a huge price tag of $10 million. Neither Dale nor I had ever raised that kind of money, but we were energized by the success we were seeing with our first thirteen tenants. We had no idea that when we started raising those millions of dollars, it would end up being the worst possible time: October 2008. Charlotte was a banking town anchored by two huge financial institutions, and the Great Recession of 2008 hit hard. Everyone worked for one of the banks or knew someone who did. While our idea was a noble one, how could we encourage donors in the midst of the worst economic crisis in decades?

Honestly, I believed our dream was dead until a small pink flutter of hope arrived in my mailbox at work. The rose-colored envelope was addressed to me. Turning it over, I saw no return address or any indication of who might have sent it. When I opened the mystery envelope and drew out the floral card inside, a few bills floated out onto the ground—a five and three ones. Inside the card, written in a shaky cursive script, the message read, "May God bless and multiply this small amount."

That was it. No name. No clue who might have sent it. Just a few dollars and a prayer that it might help our huge, impossible

$10 million dream. Those few dollars and that kind message had me smiling the rest of the day. Someone, somewhere, believed enough in our dream to build homes for the homeless to send us what seemed to be their last precious dollars and a blessing.

Given the floral card, I felt pretty certain the mysterious sender was a woman. For a moment, I even wondered if it was from my mom, who loved all things Hallmark. Mom still lived in my home-town of El Paso, Texas, and shopped at least once a week at the card shop owned by my childhood best friend, Andrea Dorsey. It was not unusual for my mom to shop at Dorsey's Cards and Gifts several times a week and mail half a dozen cards to friends and family celebrating birthdays and anniversaries. I knew, however, that the handwriting was not hers.

Two weeks passed, and the mystery faded in my memory until another card arrived. This time it was a different colored envelope and a different card, and when I opened it, a ten-dollar bill danced onto my desk. The same shaky handwriting repeated the very steady message, "May God bless and multiply this small amount."

It was an extraordinary act of faith. Who was sending us their tiny treasure in hopes it might move the million-dollar mountain before us? I could not guess. But over the next weeks and months, my Mailbox Angel was a steady groundswell of goodwill.

During the spring of 2009 and throughout the year, we would have hundreds of people, like our Mailbox Angel, begin to believe in our dream. Children held a lemonade stand on our behalf and sent us $105. A pair of Davidson College students rode their bikes across the United States to raise $6,000. There were anonymous gifts of $10,000 and one large corporate donation of $3 million. Together, the gifts became a tidal wave of generosity that finally added up to the $10 million we needed to start building our dream.

From start to finish, it took us just over four years to open the doors to Moore Place, an apartment community that would house over one hundred formerly homeless men and women at a time. Throughout those long four years, our Mailbox Angel continued sending a card with its small amount of money and blessing every two to three weeks, as if never losing hope in our dream. I could not imagine who had kept up that faithful giving all that time.

It turned out someone had been listening to their own whisper, and one of our first tenants to move into Moore Place helped us connect the God Dots.

While Dale Mullennix was the name of our longtime director of the soup kitchen, Dale Hailey was the name of one of our longtime homeless neighbors. Dale Hailey had one of the most unusual stories of all those we served at the soup kitchen. Even though he was a small man, only 5 feet 6 inches and maybe 130 pounds, he was easy to spot because of the dark-brown leather cowboy hat perched on his head. When you looked beneath the brim of his hat, you could see Dale's eyes were startlingly light blue, like sparkling aquamarines.

As a volunteer, I knew Dale Hailey from serving soup, but I didn't know his story until I started Homeless to Homes. He told me he had been a graphic designer, but when he started his career, all he needed were hand skills to use X-Acto knives and markers. When the digital age arrived with complicated design software, Dale was left behind as younger, savvier designers took his place with computers. Eventually he lost his job, which began his long landslide into homelessness.

Dale also confessed that he had never been able to sleep in the men's shelter. With more than three hundred men crowded into bunk beds at night, there was too much chaos for his gentle spirit, so he had devised his own method of survival. One day, as he wandered the railroad tracks, he had discovered a concrete platform that had been used to unload goods from the trains. While some might have decided to pitch their tent on top of this cement foundation, Dale had another idea. He dug a hole *under* the concrete, and that eight-by-eight-foot hole in the ground became his home. For years, he slept in his underground home with the concrete platform as his roof, until the day he moved into Moore Place.

While he sometimes showered at the soup kitchen, more often than not Dale had a perpetually dusty look about him from his dirt home. As soon as he moved into Moore Place, however, his transformation was remarkable. Once he was able to shower daily and sleep properly, his aquamarine eyes began to shine as if they had been polished. As he slowly reassembled the pieces of his life, Dale lost some of the shame he felt from becoming homeless and decided to reconnect with his family.

In all the years we had been serving Dale in the soup kitchen, we never knew he had family nearby, specifically a mom who loved him. She wasn't sure where her son was, but she knew he was sleeping on the streets. One day, when she was reading the local paper, she learned about our plan to build Moore Place. It started a whisper that maybe there was a way she could help.

At first it seemed like a silly idea, because she was not a wealthy woman. How could she help with a $10 million building project? That whisper, however, was insistent, and eventually she listened. She knew Moore Place might not help her son, but she had faith it might help somebody's son. She sent her prayers and her dollars, and she hoped that someday her Dale would find a home there.

And he did.

Our Mailbox Angel was Frances Hailey—Dale Hailey's mom.

We only connected those amazing God Dots by accident. Once Moore Place opened, Frances continued to send a card every few weeks to the new building but still never included her name. By that time, we had hired a professional director for Moore Place, Caroline Chambre-Hammock, who had an extensive résumé in housing.

As the new director, Caroline got to know Dale's mom because Frances had started visiting once a week to take her son grocery shopping. Although it seemed somewhat ordinary to watch a mother drive her son to the grocery store, it was extraordinary if you knew they had been separated for a decade by the chasm of homelessness. Frances and Dale were bound not only by familial love but also by genetics—they had the exact same aquamarine eyes.

One afternoon Caroline received another envelope, which she knew would contain a few dollars and a version of the "May God bless and multiply this small amount" message that had been arriving for four years. Over time, those gifts had added up to over a thousand dollars, and we still recorded them as "Anonymous." But as she tore open the latest envelope, Caroline realized this time something was different.

In the left-hand corner, opposite the postmark, it read "F. Hailey" and included a return address. After all those years, our Mailbox Angel had mistakenly told us who she was.

Caroline called me immediately. "I know who it is! All these years, all the gifts? It was Dale Hailey's mom!"

I've thought about that miracle over and over the past few years. What is the likelihood of that story? What are the chances that a woman grieving the loss of her homeless son would someday be reunited with him in part because she prayed every day to make it so? The whisper Frances Hailey heard to help Moore Place, which seemed so insignificant, turned out to be the God Dot she needed to find her son.

* * * *

The story of Frances and Dale Hailey was the first God Dot connection that, to me, was undeniable. It was beyond coincidence or chance. I could only understand it as a divine connection. Each of our stories began long before we met each other, yet they were somehow intricately woven together.

My story began with Denver Moore, which led to a quest to build Moore Place. Dale Hailey's story began with losing his job as a graphic designer and then making a long slide into homelessness that would lead to him needing a home someday. Frances Hailey's story began with listening to a whisper that she could help build such a home and then trusting her whisper for over four years.

Who could imagine that all of our whispers were part of the same story and that we would someday all be connected? To me, that is evidence of a small world connecting to a big God that resulted in huge change. In his sermon "Faith and Fiction," Frederick Buechner says it well:

> The good dream. The odd coincidence. The moment that brings tears to your eyes. The person who brings life to your life. Maybe even the smallest events hold the greatest clues. If it is God we are looking for, as I suspect all of us are, even if we don't think of it that way and wouldn't use such language on a bet, maybe the reason we haven't found him is that we are not looking in the right places.[1]

Maybe finding evidence of the divine and believing in God is as simple as paying attention. Frances had to pay attention to her whisper to send her prayers and dollars. Caroline had to pay attention to not simply throw away an outer envelope in a rush to process the card and cash she already knew would be inside. We had to pay attention to people like Dale Hailey, believing that as a human being he deserved a home and not just an eight-by-eight-foot hole in the ground.

Faith can begin as simply as that. If we are wondering where God is in our lives, perhaps we can start by noticing the holy all around us every day.

3

Betsy: A Grace Walk

Once I started paying attention, it seemed that the God Dots and the connections were everywhere. Just like the connection between Moore Place and Frances Hailey took years for me to discover, it would take time for me to understand the connection between Moore Place and my next whisper, HopeWay.

While building Moore Place was an exciting chapter in my life, it was also exhausting. For four years, it was all I had thought about. I had listened to my whisper to *Do something about it*, but now I wasn't sure what to do next.

Meeting Denver Moore had given me a story I felt I needed to tell. The miracle of building Moore Place and all its stories, like that of Frances and Dale Hailey, could not be lost. Their unimaginable happy ending needed to be remembered. I began writing down all the God Dots that had connected, if only to be sure I didn't forget them. At the time, I didn't believe it was an actual book, so I just called it my writing project.

I was planning to do some writing on a long weekend getaway to Maine I was taking with three friends: Angela Breeden, Sarah Belk, and Betsy Blue. Between the four of us we had fourteen children, so this getaway felt like a luxurious escape. We did not make a lot of plans other than to eat lobster rolls and read books.

As we waited to board our plane, Betsy said to me, "I want to talk to you about Moore Place, because Billy and I want to do something about mental health."

Angela and Sarah were longtime friends who had helped organize our True Blessings fundraiser luncheon with Denver Moore, but I did not know Betsy as well. I did know she and her husband, Bill, had a family member with bipolar disorder. Throughout my childhood, my mom had cycled in and out of the hospital with what was eventually diagnosed as bipolar disorder, and so over the years Betsy and I had several conversations about it. We had discussed how nearly impossible it was to get good mental health treatment, whether thirty years ago in Texas or in present-day North Carolina.

"Someday, we'd like to build something that could help people in Charlotte," Betsy said. She wasn't quite sure what that could be, but she had a yearning that would not go away. She recounted how she had sat at the kitchen table discussing ideas with Bill. "We talked about starting a support group, but that wouldn't solve the real need. The problem is there's no place to go for treatment."

Betsy wasn't sure what she could do to solve a problem as complex as mental health care, but she was frustrated that no one else seemed to be able to solve it either. Growing up, Betsy always secretly wanted to be an expert at something, but she just didn't know what that something was. She had gone to design school, where she learned about architectural renderings, color schemes, and interiors, and she had used that experience to work for an architect for a time, but then she chose to stay at home to raise their three children. Later she started an event planning company and had always volunteered, hoping to find that "one thing" she could excel at.

Since Betsy was an event planner and Bill was a banker, neither had any medical or psychiatric training, but they had learned a lot in the past few years through seeking treatment for someone they loved. Betsy and Bill had even been to Atlanta to tour a residential mental health model called Skyland Trail, but creating a similar program in Charlotte felt more than a little daunting. Betsy was scared to talk about what was on her heart, but the whisper to do something was not going away.

During our Maine adventure, her dream of building something became our group dream. The four of us got excited about raising money for a cause that people rarely discussed, and on our very first day we found ourselves brainstorming names of what this new place would be called.

"What about GraceRock?" Betsy asked, inspired by all the solid rock on the Maine coast. "And it is going to take a lot of God to make this happen!" And so, on our first night we raised our glasses in a toast to GraceRock—a place I am not sure any of us believed would truly appear.

On our second day, we planned to explore the Maine countryside. We wandered across the street from our inn onto the grounds of what we assumed was a beautiful park. But as we entered the iron gates, we realized it wasn't a park but some kind of campus. A small sign on the entrance explained the property was an old monastery turned into a retreat center. Down a sloping field to our right, we could see a two-story stone structure. It was an outdoor chapel, and though there was a small roof over the pulpit, the pews were on the open lawn.

Venturing down the hill toward the chapel, we saw the sunlight was streaming through a window and illuminating the altar, which was covered with candles, rosaries, letters, and flowers. Dozens of visitors before us had left small offerings to God. As we silently explored the chapel, Betsy was drawn to a particular letter held down on the altar by flat gray stones.

Betsy began reading it at the altar, and then she took the pages with her to a pew. Her shoulders rounded forward, and the sunlight touched the top of her head, making it almost glow. She appeared to cradle the letter in her lap as if to protect the story she had just discovered. Watching Betsy, I realized tears were sliding down her cheeks.

Angela, Sarah, and I gathered around to find out what was making her cry. "It's a letter from a mom begging for help," Betsy said.

The pages she found had been typed by a mom who had a daughter with mental health issues. The young girl was a runaway, and the mother had no idea how to find her. Page after page, the story poured out in painful, pleading sentences written by a mom who no doubt loved her child as much as we loved ours.

"This is why we have to do this!" Betsy said. "There are too many people and nowhere for them to go for help!"

We all knew what Betsy meant. She was talking about our imaginary GraceRock and the whisper she and Bill were hearing to *Do something about it*. This letter felt like more than coincidence. It felt like divine intervention, a confirmation just in case Betsy was not convinced she should listen to her whisper. Of all the dozens of items on the altar, this mother's specific plea found its way into Betsy's hands.

"It's still so wild to me that with all that was going on inside me to do something, I find that letter," Betsy said. "It really was a God thing."

Before that letter, all of our scheming about building a mental health treatment center had just been talk—four friends dreaming dreams that made for fun brainstorming. I hadn't believed much would happen when we returned home, though perhaps Bill and Betsy would do something.

Until I saw her crying over that letter, I had no whisper of my own. Watching Betsy weep in the stone chapel, however, I felt like many threads in my own story were pulled tight at that moment. Maybe I was not just supposed to simply be talking about Bill and Betsy's dream. Maybe I was supposed to help do something about it too.

During my childhood, I remember missing my mom when she was hospitalized for psychiatric treatment. There had been nothing in El Paso like the beautiful, restorative GraceRock we imagined. More often than not, my mom received treatment in locked wards of hospitals that were designed for mending broken bodies, not broken minds. Often it seemed Mom came home more shattered than healed.

What if we could create a holistic mental health wellness center in Charlotte? Maybe that was why I had worked so hard to learn how to build Moore Place—so that I could help Bill and Betsy with their own dream.

When we returned home from our trip, Betsy told Bill and her daughter, Nancy, all about our weekend brainstorming, but Nancy didn't think GraceRock was the right name. "HopeWay," Nancy told her mom. "Call it HopeWay. Because even when it seems like you have lost everything, you can still find a way to hope."

Two weeks after our Maine adventure, Betsy called me and said, "I know this is premature, but I think there is a property we could buy. Do you want to come look at it with us?" Apparently, Bill had mentioned the very preliminary plans for HopeWay to a commercial real estate broker.

"It's a little early," Bill admitted. "But someday we want to build a treatment center, so let me know if you ever see a property that might work."

"Funny you say that," the broker told him. "I just got a new listing, and I think it might be exactly what you need."

The listing turned out to be a twelve-acre property that not only had all the makings of a mental health wellness center but miraculously was already properly zoned. Originally built as an alcohol treatment center, the 52,000-square-foot building had been renovated and was being used as a private school. As we toured the campus, which included a gymnasium and wooded walking trails, it didn't take much imagination to see how it could become the HopeWay dream. It was absolutely perfect, but the asking price was $7 million.

"Where are we going to find that kind of money?" Betsy asked.

The real question was, Where would we ever find that kind of property again? Despite the daunting price, we all agreed there was something miraculous at work in the timing.

To Betsy, not only was the timing divine but something else about the property was as well. It was built in 1988, the same year her first daughter was born. "There were just so many signs along the way," Betsy said. "That was another one for me. Once we found that property, I never had any doubt. I knew we were going to do this."

A few weeks later, eight of us gathered in Bill and Betsy's living room to consider the audacious goal of buying the property and creating a world-class mental health treatment center. None of us had professional psychiatric or medical experience, but each one of us had a personal connection to the cause. We knew how difficult it was to find care. This would become the very first official meeting of the newly formed HopeWay Foundation.

As I left Bill and Betsy's home that night, I knew somehow that these remarkable God Dots were going to start connecting into something extraordinary. There was a feeling in that room that was undeniable. Something about Bill and Betsy's passion was contagious. Even if it turned out to be impossible, we all knew we had to try—it felt crazier not to.

For Betsy, that night was the beginning of having no doubt HopeWay would one day become a reality. "I think it was meant to happen, and we were the ones who were in the position to make it happen," she said. "God put that on our hearts. I think he puts people in our lives to be the hands and feet we need."

None of us understood all that it would take, but everything Betsy had learned in her life, from understanding mental health to interior design to event planning, was about to come together.

"I knew it was my purpose," she said. "And my purpose found me."

4

Dru: Remembering Mitch

After that first meeting in Bill and Betsy's living room, our small group of eight expanded to twelve and became HopeWay's first board of directors. As our first step toward building, we each donated resources to gather enough money to put that twelve-acre property under contract. Then we outlined a full fundraising plan for the money needed to transform the former school into Charlotte's first residential mental health treatment center.

Many of the features Betsy had talked about on our Maine getaway began coming to life. The blueprints included a dining hall, therapy rooms, a meditation room, an art center, a learning kitchen, a horticulture lab, gardens, and a gymnasium. HopeWay was becoming exactly what Bill and Betsy had dreamed of, but it was also much more expensive than anyone had imagined.

Once all the architectural plans were made, we realized it would take more than $25 million to complete. That kind of money meant corporate donations and foundation grants, which would take months to get—not to mention a lot of convincing to back a board with big dreams but no professional psychiatrists, therapists, or other medical professionals. We decided we would have to start with people just like us—those who understood what it was like to not to be able to find help. Beginning with friends who had experienced a mental health crisis in their own families, and branching out from there as we formed connections, we started having a thousand cups of coffee to raise the money.

One afternoon I met with a woman named Dru Dougherty Abrams who understood the deep impact of mental health struggles. Her son Mitch had paranoid schizophrenia disorder and died by suicide ten days before his twenty-second birthday. Although she was divorced, Dru and her ex-husband, Rick, had reconciled, coming back to live as a family to help parent Mitch.

"I think God facilitated that," Dru told me later. "I can't imagine how I could have navigated that by myself."

Rick had heard about the plans for HopeWay from Bill Blue. "Rick and I were so hopeful that HopeWay could be an option for Mitch," Dru said. "We were devastated that Mitch died before he could take advantage of the program."

Because of that, Dru and Rick had asked that donations in Mitch's memory be designated for HopeWay. Shortly after the funeral, Dru asked to meet in person about making a family donation to HopeWay. Because I had become the volunteer development director for HopeWay, I found myself sitting across from Dru in a café with our coffee steaming silently between us. With beautiful soft, white-blond curls framing a face full of sorrow, Dru stared down at her cup. I wasn't sure how to start a conversation with a grieving stranger, so I began with the only sentence that came to mind.

"Tell me about Mitch," I said.

Dru looked up at me suddenly, as if I had startled her awake. For a moment I was afraid I'd said exactly the wrong thing, because her eyes welled with tears. But then the corners of her sad lips turned up into a smile.

"Oh, thank you," she said. "Thank you for saying his name. Everyone is afraid to say Mitch's name around me."

Smiling back in embarrassment and relief, I knew it wasn't wisdom or kindness that made me say it. I simply didn't know how else to begin.

"People think if they say his name it triggers painful memories," Dru said. "But it's not like I don't think about him every minute of every day."

Neither of us spoke for a moment.

"But I don't want to forget," she added. "I want to remember."

We began talking about Mitch, whom Dru told me was one of four sons. That part of her story struck me; she had four sons and I had four daughters. As we talked, I learned about Mitch's struggle with schizophrenia and how, throughout his teens, Dru and Rick had tried to get their son all the mental health care he needed. Often Mitch refused to take his prescribed medications, not believing he had a problem. Over time, he started self-medicating with other substances, but it was the schizophrenia more than the addictions that was his toughest battle.

"We told Mitch that as long as he took his medication, we would pay his rent, but often he wouldn't," she told me. Dru and Rick knew the stakes were high. If Mitch continued to be medically noncompliant, he could become a danger to himself and others.

"When he refused to take his medicines, Mitch became homeless," Dru admitted.

That was somehow shocking to me. Even after years of working with people who experienced homelessness, it was still surprising to understand not all stories were linked to extreme poverty. Dru seemed to understand the connection I was making, that her homeless son came from a family of means.

"Mitch used to get help sometimes at the soup kitchen," she said. I must have looked surprised because Dru nodded, letting me know that she was aware I had worked there.

This was the first time I spoke with someone who was impacted by both the Roof Above soup kitchen and what HopeWay would become. It also occurred to me that I might have met Mitch while serving soup over the years. Had I handed him a meal tray, never thinking about whether, like Frances and Dale Hailey, Mitch also had a mom who loved him but just didn't know how to help him?

As we continued to sip our drinks, Dru and I talked about the intersection of homelessness and mental health. While there was overlap, not everyone who became homeless was mentally ill and not everyone who had mental health issues became homeless. Even where similarities existed, every individual story was different. After a deep discussion, Dru brought us back to why she had asked to meet.

"The real reason we want to give to HopeWay in memory of Mitch is because of the gym," Dru said.

"The gym?" I asked, not quite sure what she meant.

"Yes, the gym on the back of your new property," Dru said. "When it was a school, they used to rent out the gym, and Mitch played AAU basketball there all the time."

Dru seemed to light up as she remembered Mitch playing ball, but I couldn't speak. The thought of her once healthy and athletic son shooting hoops in a gym before schizophrenia derailed his life made me start to cry. For a few moments, we just held silent space together. Even before I understood the significance, Dru had already made the God Dot connection.

"I couldn't believe that the same place Mitch loved playing basketball might now become the type of place that could have saved him," Dru said.

It was difficult for me to believe that as well. The place she remembered as being part of Mitch's happiest memories was now going to be a place that helped heal people just like him.

"That's why we want to be a part of HopeWay," she said.

Since she had not been able to save her own son, Dru, along with her family and friends, gave all they could to help other people's children—just like Frances Hailey had done for her son.

That became the miracle of HopeWay. We started by meeting with a small circle of friends whom we knew had mental health issues in their family, and they would typically end a meeting by connecting us to others. Each family we met would have given anything to help their mothers, fathers, sisters, brothers, husbands, or wives who had experienced mental health challenges. For some, like Dru, it was already too late to help the one they loved, so they gave all they could to HopeWay.

From thousand-dollar personal gifts to seven-figure foundation grants, the generosity we received was astounding. In only three years, we raised over $27 million, completed renovations on the facilities, and planned a grand opening.

While Bill had been the business force behind HopeWay, Betsy had been the vision keeper. She knew exactly what would transform the old school into a place of healing. Working with the architects, Betsy and a small group of volunteers had overseen every finish, every fabric, and every detail to make HopeWay a sanctuary where people could recover and feel restored. All of her history came together, and Betsy had finally become an expert at something: making HopeWay into exactly the kind of place everyone would want to bring their own child, parent, or loved one to receive healing.

At the grand opening, there were hugs, tears, and wonder all around. For the first time in my life, I was almost grateful I had grown up with a mom who had a mental health challenge, because everyone was there together for the same reason. None of us would have worked so hard for HopeWay if we did not have the painful memories of watching someone we loved suffer.

"This feels like church," one donor told me, offering a huge embrace. "Isn't this what church is supposed to feel like?"

Betsy felt overwhelming gratitude for all the friends and family who had jumped on board. "Mental health can be so lonely," she said. "But none of us were alone anymore. It was all out in the open and we had done something about it."

How could a couple with no medical or psychiatric background turn an impossible dream into this reality? It had started with Betsy and Bill's whisper, but it became a collective whisper.

As we celebrated, the halls were filled with sunflowers, balloons, and live music, but more importantly, the new center was overflowing with hope. After thousands of volunteer hours and hundreds of helping hands, we were standing in the reality of what happens when you listen to a whisper and all the God Dots connect.

"Everything just seemed to fall into place," Betsy said. "There were never any true roadblocks, because it all just came together."

. . . .

A year after that grand opening there was another celebration, called "Hoops for HopeWay." It was a fundraiser cochaired by Dru Dougherty Abrams. Teams signed up to compete in a three-on-three basketball tournament to raise not only money but awareness about mental health.

"It brought together not only Mitch's love of the game but also involved some groups reluctant to discuss mental health, like men and those in minority communities," Dru said.

She admits the event was also important for her own healing. "After a suicide, you are just desperate to make some meaning out of such a tragedy," she said. "Being involved with HopeWay felt like a lifeline."

The event was held in the HopeWay gym, where there is a sign on the wall that reads, "The Mitch Abrams Basketball Court, generously gifted by the Abrams family and friends in celebration of the life of Mitch Abrams."

Dru's three other sons came to the event, and it felt to her as if all four of her boys were together. "I felt a real sense of peace that day," she said. "Mitch was there too."

5

Beverly: Airplane Angel

As we worked on raising money for HopeWay, I was also finishing my writing project. The stories of Denver Moore and Frances Hailey, our Mailbox Angel, were coming together as part of a full-length book. Dale Mullennix, the executive director of the soup kitchen, had asked me if I would tell some of those stories at that year's True Blessings. Since it was the fifth anniversary of when Denver Moore had spoken, Dale thought it would be very "full circle" if I was the keynote speaker.

While I agreed with him that the stories from building Moore Place were powerful, I wasn't sure I was the right person to tell them. This was a thousand-person event in a ballroom with a stage, lights, and high expectations for a presentation I did not feel qualified to deliver. I politely declined his invitation, but Dale did not want to take no for an answer. He called me into his office to try to convince me to change my mind. I think that because he was a former Baptist minister, Dale believed he could put a little higher-power pressure on me during our conversation.

"I know you don't want to do this, but God keeps telling me you are supposed to be the speaker this year," he said with utter conviction.

"Well, honestly, I haven't heard God talking to me about it, so I am okay telling you no," I told him with a smile.

Dale looked at me over his thick black glasses and frowned into his graying mustache. We seemed to be at a stalemate.

Before I left his office, Dale tried one last tactic. He handed me a book by Bruce Wilkinson titled *You Were Born for This: Seven Keys to a Life of Predictable Miracles*.

"It's about how we often miss everyday miracles happening all around us," Dale said. "But really, it's about how we can all be a part of them."

Opening the bright orange book, I read the first lines:

What if I told you I'm certain you missed a miracle yesterday? And not just any miracle but one Heaven wanted to do through you to significantly change someone's life for the better—maybe even your own?[1]

Wilkinson was writing about noticing when God nudges us to do something and being willing to act on it. Although I had never heard of him, the cover informed me he also was the bestselling author of *The Prayer of Jabez*. *Funny*, I thought, *two bestselling books, but I've never heard of this guy*. I wasn't sure why Dale thought this book would change my mind, but I promised him I would read it.

Two weeks later, I was on a nine-hour plane journey from North Carolina to California to meet some friends for a reunion. Along with my laptop and lots of work, I had packed Dale's book, which I had almost finished. While it had not convinced me to stand at a podium in front of a thousand people, I had to admit it was a compelling read.

On my second flight, from Dallas to Los Angeles, I squeezed into my window seat beside a silver-haired woman who was quietly knitting in the middle seat. She had a pleasant calmness about her, and at another time I might have struck up a conversation. On this flight, however, I planned to finish a homework assignment for a writing class I was taking through a local college.

As we buckled our seat belts and prepared for takeoff, I happened to make eye contact with the nice knitter beside me. She did not say a word as she smiled back, but I distinctly heard a whisper when I looked at her. *Ask her what she does.*

Lowering my eyes, I consciously ignored this suggestion. Ironically, I had just read about exactly this type of experience; Bruce Wilkinson wrote of several instances on planes where small miracles had occurred through unlikely connections and this type of God nudge. I dismissed the whisper I'd heard as just a figment of my imagination due to the power of suggestion from reading that book. I didn't have time to test the author's theory on God nudges on this flight. The only miracle I needed was to finish my homework before the deadline.

During the entire three-hour flight, I successfully avoided speaking with my seatmate and furiously typed on my laptop. With only twenty minutes remaining, I completed the assignment.

That's when the whisper began again: *Ask her what she does.*

Why was this happening? My seatmate was nice enough, but what could a woman who was knitting and most likely retired possibly have to tell me about what she does?

I tried looking out the window, hoping the whisper would go away, but it came again. *Ask her what she does.*

It was undeniably insistent, so I knew I was going to have to listen. Turning to the woman, I tried an easy opening line about the airport where our flight began.

"You live near Dallas?" I asked.

"Yes," she said, not looking up from her knitting.

Maybe she wasn't interested in talking to me either. But in his book, Wilkinson suggested that, when you found people you were inexplicably drawn to meet, you try asking different questions to understand why.

"Where are you going in California?" I asked, hoping for a clue about why we might need to be talking.

"Um, I don't actually know," she said. "Someone is picking me up at the airport and then driving me to a conference."

She must have seen my face. Who signs up for a conference but doesn't know where they are going?

"I'm speaking at the conference, so they are driving me," she explained.

There it was. The answer to *Ask her what she does*. Apparently, of all things, my silver-haired knitting seatmate was a speaker. I could feel a full-body tingle run through me as if to say, *Told you so! This is important. Pay attention.*

"What do you speak about?" I asked, more than a little curious where this conversation might be headed.

"I travel all over the country for Al-Anon. I have been doing it for years," she said. "I try to help others."

This was starting to feel like more than a coincidence or some sweet serendipity. Was this another divine appointment?

"Did you ever imagine you would become a speaker?" I asked.

The woman shook her head. "Never! It was all God. If you had told me years ago I would be traveling all over the United States and Canada speaking, I never would have believed you."

By now I was sweating, and I felt the need to confess.

"It's funny you say that, because I am trying to write a book and someone just asked me to speak about it," I told her. "It's about feeling called to work on homelessness, but I am afraid to talk about it."

The kind woman seemed to be listening intently even as I kept rambling, as though she were patiently waiting for me to get to a question.

"I'm just trying to get comfortable with it all—"

"Don't!" she interrupted. "Don't *ever* get comfortable with it! If you do, then it becomes about you and not about God."

I must have looked a bit shocked to have a stranger tell me this, but she continued. "When you become comfortable, it becomes about your ego and not God. Most of the time, when I stand up, I never know what I am going to say," she said. "When you become comfortable with it, you need to quit and do something else."

How could she be saying this?

How could this woman know exactly the words I needed to hear? I hadn't planned to start speaking any more than I had planned to house the homeless, but it seemed that both were inevitable.

"The most important thing you need to do before you talk is pray," she said confidently. "Before I speak, I go into a bathroom stall, and I pray that I say God's words and not mine. Then, when I speak, sometimes I feel like my mouth is moving and I don't even know what is coming out."

My eyes filled with tears as she spoke. *Ask her what she does.*

Why that whisper? How could anyone have known? In all the planes taking off and landing all across the country, why would this woman, a *speaker*, be sitting next to me? She was exactly the person I needed to meet in exactly the right moment, and I had almost let her leave without asking what she does.

I had almost let my miracle go unnoticed and unrevealed.

Placing my hand on her arm, I tried to convey what an extraordinary meeting this was for me.

"Thank you. You have no idea how I needed to hear what you are saying," I said. "I had this odd whisper I should ask you what you do, and I almost didn't."

She nodded, understanding as much as I did that we were meant to speak together. This was, without a doubt, a conversation I was destined to have, just like my meeting with Denver.

Leaning in close, she said, "You will notice your hands will get cold sometimes before you speak. I have been told that is because everything goes to your heart. You want to speak from your heart always."

I had the sudden urge to grab a pen and write down every word she said. The other passengers were now getting off the plane, but I hadn't even noticed that we had landed.

"Good luck," she said, gathering her bag, but I didn't want to let her go. I needed to be sure she had told me everything she knew.

"Do you have a card?" I asked as we followed each other into the terminal.

As we put our bags down, she searched her purse to find a pale green business card and handed it to me. I read the name of my airplane angel: Beverly Burnett.

Beverly grabbed my hand to say goodbye. "Don't forget the most important thing to do before you speak is to pray. Anything you like is fine. The Lord's Prayer, anything," she said, and then she added, "My favorite is the prayer of Jabez."

My heart stopped when Beverly said *the prayer of Jabez*. It was the prayer I'd never heard of, yet it was the title of that other best-selling book by Bruce Wilkinson. The guy who believed we could all be a part of small daily miracles if we only just paid attention.

"You have no idea," I told her, hugging her tightly. "You were an angel to me today."

As I walked to the baggage claim, I replayed it all in my head. Once my bag had arrived, I sat down and wrote out every holy word Beverly had just given me. Then I called Dale Mullennix.

"If you haven't already booked another speaker, I will do it," I said.

"God finally talking to you?" Dale asked.

"Yes." I smiled. "God is definitely talking to me."

6

Caroline: The Simple Solution

By the time I finished my writing project about Moore Place, it had taken nearly five years to complete. Rereading the stories in the final manuscript, I couldn't find the right title, and nothing seemed to fit. One day, my friend Julie Marr, also a writer, texted me these words:

The Hundred Story Home

She didn't have to write another word. It was as if that was already the title of my book, and it was meant to be.

Although I now had a finished manuscript with the perfect title, I couldn't find a publisher interested in my story of building homes for the homeless and all the God Dots that had aligned to make it a reality. So, after multiple rejections, I decided to self-publish the book just so I could finally honor my whisper to *Write it down*. It felt important to say and to share what had happened. In truth, Moore Place had never been my idea. It was Denver Moore's idea, and I needed to bear witness to the whisper he'd started. The whole project and all those who helped—we were all part of something much bigger.

I could not be certain, but it felt like the whisper to write it down was part of something much bigger as well. Maybe there were other people hearing whispers to *Do something* they felt unqualified for. If they read *The Hundred Story Home*, maybe it could help give them courage to follow their whisper. I kept telling myself there were surely at least ten people out there who were hearing their own whispers, so my book needed to find its way to those ten readers.

How was I going to find those strangers? I had no idea how to be an author or market a book, so I asked around for recommendations on how to understand social media. The last time I had used Facebook was for my high school reunion, and I had no idea how to post, like, or comment. A friend suggested I talk with Corri Smith, who had her own marketing company. When I met with her, I shared my hopes that my book would find readers who needed courage for their own whispers. Corri had a brilliant idea for how we could spread this story to people in cities beyond Charlotte: Little Free Libraries.

Corri explained that those dollhouse-like boxes in front of people's homes were one way booklovers share books. She could create an Instagram "scavenger hunt," and we would place a copy of *The Hundred Story Home* in ten Little Free Libraries in ten Southern cities to give away a total of one hundred copies.

When she researched the Little Free Library network, Corri discovered a listing of "owners" of these libraries and began contacting them by email. We didn't have a very scientific approach. We just randomly picked names, hoping they might be willing to help a rookie author.

One of the emails Corri sent was to a woman named Rachel Estes in Birmingham, Alabama. When Rachel read the message from a stranger in Charlotte about *The Hundred Story Home*, she realized this might be something more important than an Instagram contest.

Rachel wrote back that she would be happy to help us, but for her, it was bigger than that.

This is a chill bump connection!

I'm director of outreach and missions at Canterbury United Methodist Church . . . so literally my days are filled with connecting people in the congregation with their passions and the community's needs, from homelessness to prison ministry to tutoring, etc.

So, at the risk of sounding a little wacky, I'm a great person to get this book into hands of folks looking, praying, and thinking about homelessness.

Reading Rachel's email, I felt another full-body tingle, and I shook my head at the coincidence. What were the chances that our email would land in the inbox of someone so missionally aligned with my book? Over the next few months, Rachel became my inspirational pen pal, sending stories of friends she had shared the book with. After several email exchanges, Rachel invited me to be a guest speaker at her church, which made me feel both excited and terrified.

My God Dot connection with Beverly Burnett on the plane had convinced me to speak in Charlotte for the True Blessings event, but I still was not confident about talking in front of people. I had been trying to follow Beverly's advice to remember to make it about God and not about me. Each time I spoke at a book club or church in Charlotte, I went into the bathroom first and said a little prayer that usually ended with, "God, I will show up if you will show off." Even with this ritual, I still felt nauseated and would sweat through my blouse by the end of my presentation.

If I accepted Rachel's offer in Birmingham, it would be the first time someone had asked me to travel to deliver a message. The weight of that expectation felt enormous. What did I know about speaking? What could I possibly say to a church group? But with all of her wisdom and experience, Rachel had a faith in me that I didn't have in myself. And so, I went.

Getting into Rachel's car at the Birmingham airport, I was so nervous I thought I might be sick. She was so excited to meet an "author" in person, but I didn't feel like a real author. Weren't "real authors" the people with agents and publishing contracts who were booked on morning talk shows?

Rachel didn't seem to know or care about any of that—she just loved my book. As we drove to her church, Rachel gave me an overview of the schedule ahead and the people I would be meeting.

"Caroline Bundy is beside herself to talk with you," she said. "I think she may have a whisper."

Caroline Bundy was a member at Rachel's church, and her wife, Valerie, was the director of senior adult ministries. Months before, Rachel had pressed a copy of *The Hundred Story Home* into Caroline's hands and told her, "You have to read this."

As it turned out, Caroline really did. She had been hearing her own whisper for quite a while. One that was inconvenient, unexpected, and uncomfortable. While her day job was as the development director for a nonprofit called AIDS Alabama, Caroline's whisper was not directly related to her career. What broke Caroline's heart was the complicated problem of runaway teens trapped in sex trafficking.

When Caroline and I met for breakfast, I learned much more of her story. She grew up in Montgomery, Alabama, the youngest of four children, but she had been raised more like an only child because her siblings were so much older. Even when she was young, Caroline knew the problem of homelessness bothered her in a way that felt different from her friends.

"At Halloween, when kids would dress up as 'hobos,' all dirty with a bandanna on a stick, I didn't like it," she said. "I knew it wasn't right, and I felt sorry for those men who jumped trains and slept in the woods."

Growing up, Caroline was never sure what she wanted to be. "My mom always said I would be a good lawyer because I loved to argue!" she told me.

But after graduating from the University of Alabama with a BA in communications, Caroline still felt her path was unclear. She described what she called her "broken road," a long series of jobs that led her to where she was now. That path included working at a weekly newspaper, in real estate, as a restaurant manager, in wholesale wine sales, and even co-owning a specialty food business with Valerie. She'd found her way into the nonprofit world first as the program director for the YMCA in Birmingham and then through raising money for AIDS Alabama.

It was at that nonprofit, working with a colleague on a program called the Ascension Project, that she first began to understand the needs of young adults experiencing homelessness and heard a whisper to *Do something about it*. As Caroline spoke, she ran her fingers through her wavy brown hair, looking at me with earnest desperation.

"I feel crazy," she told me. "This idea just won't leave me, but I don't know how I could possibly do it."

Caroline's insistent whisper was not exactly about housing; it was about runaway teens.

"They come on the bus to Birmingham from all over Alabama to escape bad situations at home, but they know no one," she told me. "The traffickers prey on these kids by offering them help, but they are just trapping them. Within hours after arriving at the bus station, these poor kids are lost into the sex trafficking system."

She rolled off some statistics about the need, and I could tell Caroline had been studying the problem. These young adults needed so many things to create stable lives: housing skills, job skills, financial literacy. She had so much empathy for these kids who left what they knew for the dream of something better yet ended up in a nightmare.

"If you don't have love and support at home, how in the world do you ever get past that?" Caroline said. She had deep admiration for the teens finding the courage to overcome unsupportive and traumatic childhoods.

"What I keep thinking about is that the solution is so easy," she said. "We just need to put a shelter with services for these teens right next to that bus station. If we did that, then *we* would be the first people these kids meet, not those sex traffickers."

Caroline's idea was so brilliantly simple, yet, at the same time, so complex. Like Moore Place and HopeWay, her idea would require a lot of time, money, and community support to make it happen.

"I even have the name for it," Caroline said. "It would be called 'The Way Station.'"

By the time she told me all this over breakfast, it turned out she'd already written two grants asking for money for the Way Station and had received both of them. Now she had an idea and some funding, but there was still a long road ahead. When Rachel had given her *The Hundred Story Home*, Caroline felt like it was the God Dot she needed to listen to her own whisper.

After a long "broken road," Caroline was finally becoming exactly who she was meant to be and beginning the project she was born to do. Over the next few months, we emailed several times, and Caroline kept me updated on her progress. It was a bigger task than she had imagined.

"If I had known what it was going to grow to be, I am not sure I would have done it," Caroline admitted to me later.

In order to fully serve the young adults who needed help, the Way Station would grow to become a 15,000-square-foot building with room for forty, including an emergency shelter and longer-term transitional housing. It would also be a 24/7 operation with three eight-hour shifts of employees providing counseling and life skills as well as three meals a day. It was going to be much more complicated than a "simple solution," yet at the same time it *was* simple. These kids needed help, and someone needed to care enough to help them. Caroline Bundy became that someone.

It took more than six years to raise the necessary $4.2 million and work through the development, construction, and licensing hurdles. The global pandemic would delay progress for almost two years, but Caroline Bundy finally helped cut the red ribbon on her whisper in 2022. More than three hundred donors had helped fund the Way Station, and the mayor showed up to deliver remarks at the grand opening. Caroline remembers pure elation from that day and saying over and over to herself in amazement, *We did it!*

· · · ·

It was dark by the time all the invited guests left, and after Caroline finished cleaning up from the ceremony, she collapsed into a lounge chair in the courtyard of the Way Station. She looked up at the stars above her, shining as if in a celestial celebration of her long journey. So many times over the past six years she had wondered if they would make it or if she was losing her mind to think she could do this.

That heavenly sky felt like confirmation that Caroline had never lost anything. Her whisper had been the beginning of being holy *found*.

7

Meg: The Tai Chi Studio Windowsill

Caroline Bundy became the first of many more whisper stories as *The Hundred Story Home* kept finding its way into the hands of readers who needed it. Every week I received emails and texts from friends who wanted either to discuss their own whisper or to have me speak to a group about homelessness. It was as if a mysterious force was swirling beneath the pages to reveal God Dot connections like Caroline Bundy and the Way Station.

That is why I was not terribly surprised to open an early-morning email from Liz Clasen-Kelly telling me about a friend of hers who had read the book. Liz, a central character in *The Hundred Story Home*, had been the assistant director of the soup kitchen and was the first person in Charlotte to passionately advocate for a Housing First program. She wrote:

> I just got an email from a volunteer whose aunt in Buffalo sent her your book. How cool is that? I'd love to see the equivalent of a flight

map showing the arrows of how people find your book. Each would have its own story.

Reading Liz's message about a "flight map" made me smile, and I also knew who she might be talking about. That same week, I had received an email from a woman named Meg Robertson, who asked to meet. While I had met with several readers in Charlotte who were friends or acquaintances, Meg was the first total stranger who wanted to have coffee with me.

Arriving at the café a bit early, I chose a high-top table near the front door so we would not miss each other. I purposely placed a copy of *The Hundred Story Home* beside my vanilla latte to be sure Meg could recognize me. I was so curious to hear the full story about receiving a copy of the book from her aunt in Buffalo. Her email had read:

> My aunt Mary found it on the windowsill of the place she goes for tai chi. It was mixed in with the free magazines and looked like an interesting read, so she read it, gave it to my mom, and said, "Please give this to Meg when you're done. They are two peas in a pod. I'm sure Meg probably knows her."

That made me laugh—the book was found on a tai chi studio windowsill mixed in with the free magazines? And why were we "two peas in a pod"? I could not wait to find out.

A fortyish woman with shoulder-length, red hair opened the glass door, and when she saw me, her face broke into an immediate smile as if we were old high school friends. I know now that in some ways this was true. Meg and I might have been strangers that afternoon, but I believe we were meant to become lifelong friends.

Time passed quickly as we realized all the ways we should have met before. Meg had lived in Charlotte for twenty years, worked for Habitat for Humanity for almost a decade, and also served meals at the men's shelter for years. We discovered we knew many of the same people, volunteered at the same places, and focused on much of the same work. As we discussed all our points of connection, it was remarkable that we had never crossed paths.

"So, your aunt Mary found my book on the windowsill of a tai chi studio?" I asked.

Meg laughed as she said, "Crazy, right?"

"But how did it get to there?" I wondered. "It's only self-published, so how did it get to upstate New York?"

Raising her eyebrows, Meg looked at me funny.

"I thought you put it there," she said.

"I have never even been to Buffalo, and definitely not to a tai chi studio there," I told her.

"But I thought you wrote on my copy?" As she spoke, she reached into her bag to pull out the book that had somehow made its way from Charlotte to Buffalo and then into her hands.

Meg handed me a copy of my book with its light-blue cover. There was handwriting in thick black marker along the sides that was not mine. The top edge read "Not for Sale," and along the long edge it read "Always a Gift."

Meg watched my face as I read those words for the first time. "You didn't write that?"

I shook my head, trying to imagine who did, and how this book had traveled so far. Liz Clasen-Kelly was right about the flight map idea; this copy had definitely been on a journey.

"So, you don't know about this either?" she asked opening the inside cover.

There, in the same black marker handwriting, it read:

This book was donated by the author. After reading it,
please share it with others and drop a note to the author.

And it listed my website to contact me.

"You didn't write that?" Meg asked.

"No, I've never seen this," I told her. "So, this is why you emailed me?"

"Yes! I was following these instructions that I thought *you* wrote!"

We studied the book together, trying to solve the puzzle. It was quite the mysterious God Dot to connect, and neither of us knew how to make sense of it. But by the time we ended our two-hour coffee conversation, Meg and I both felt it was just the beginning of a friendship. Her aunt had been right—we were two peas in a pod. After all our remarkable connections and the strange way we had finally met over a book placed mysteriously on a tai chi studio windowsill, there was a whisper telling me Meg was supposed to be in my life.

At the time, I didn't know she was listening to her own whisper—one she was afraid to tell me about so soon, since we barely knew each other. Long before I wrote about listening to whispers in *The Hundred Story Home*, she had been following her own God nudges. Born in upstate New York, Meg spent fourteen years with her family in the Midwest before they moved back to Buffalo when she was sixteen. When she started high school at an all-girls Catholic school, she felt like an outsider among the teens who all seemed wealthier and much more sophisticated.

In early November, Meg began to hear an odd whisper that she should help feed people for Thanksgiving in her new community. It did not make much sense. She was only a teenager. What could she do about hunger?

One day in the cafeteria, Meg had an even stranger thought about her classmates: *I bet even the loose change in their pockets could feed a lot of people.*

She became very excited about the idea, and asked a teacher, Ms. Podd, for permission to collect loose change to feed hungry families. Every day, Meg walked around school asking her classmates for their spare change to buy Thanksgiving dinners for those who would otherwise go hungry that holiday. Eventually, Meg collected over three hundred dollars, and Ms. Podd drove Meg to the grocery store to buy turkeys and deliver them to a nonprofit that would distribute them to families in the community.

"I don't know what made me think of that," Meg told me later on. "But it felt amazing that so many families would have Thanksgiving dinner just because I had collected spare change."

It was the first whisper Meg could remember hearing, and after that one, there were many more.

By the time she met me for coffee, Meg had already listened to whispers that insisted she should walk the Appalachian Trail, build houses with Habitat for Humanity, and cook meals at the men's shelter. She said that sometimes the ideas felt more like an inner knowing she should do something rather than actual plans.

Only after we knew each other better did she confess that she also received messages she was certain she was meant to pass along. She wasn't sure how to explain it, but it was as if she received divine messages for others and was simply the human who delivered them. In fact, that was the real reason Meg had asked to meet with me in person. While reading my book, Meg felt she'd received a direct message—one meant for me.

Since my contact information was written inside her copy of the book, this only amplified her very specific whisper. She'd planned to tell me the message the first time we met. Meg had even told her husband (a practical police officer) and her best friend about it, both of whom lovingly advised her not to say anything to me. While they both understood the messages Meg sometimes received and believed her, they doubted a stranger would understand.

"Kathy will definitely think you are insane if you tell her," her friend advised. "Just wait until she knows you better before you say anything."

During our coffee, Meg listened to that advice, but the very next day she sent me a long email. When I read it, I was on a plane traveling to a planned summer vacation. At the end, she wrote about a specific passage in my book she had been reading when she received a direct message for me.

> Finally, at the risk of sounding creepy, you wrote about how you regretted not telling your dad [before he died]:

> "You are the best, Dad!" I should've said, "You were always there for me, Dad. No matter what happened to Mom, I always knew I would never be left alone."

> He knew Kathy. He knows. He's still with you in spirit, and he's always known. I cried when I read that section, because I KNOW he knows, and I felt I needed to tell you that.

That was the part that made me cry. That was the part that stopped my heart. The words felt like they were sent straight from heaven and made me forever grateful to the God Dots that connected my book to a Buffalo tai chi studio windowsill, to Meg, and to her message miraculously finding its way to me.

I wrote back to Meg, telling her how much it meant to me and that her message made me cry, really weep, on a plane. Meg wrote back:

> Sorry I made you cry. It needed to be said. I felt it so strongly and fiercely when I read that page. I also felt a sense of urgency around telling you, like I owed it to your dad. I know that's odd, because clearly, I've never met him.

My dad had died two decades before Meg and I met. I carried a secret regret that he had not been alive to see both Moore Place and HopeWay. Dad was the real reason I wanted to do something that mattered and leave the world a better place. He was why I had that folder in my desk labeled "Change the World."

Although he worked as a lawyer, my dad was a minister at heart. He had attended seminary for a year before leaving to go to law school. I was never sure why he decided not to become a minister, but service remained a central part of his life. He was a deacon at our church and volunteered at local nonprofits, including the El Paso Cancer Foundation. Although he helped lead their annual fundraiser, I doubt my dad ever imagined he would be a cancer patient himself. Yet at only sixty-four years old, Dad died from complications of Acute Myeloid Leukemia (AML), leaving a long bucket list of adventures not taken and four granddaughters he would never fully know.

Because my father died with so much left undone, it accelerated my search to find what I was meant to do in this world. I would not begin to find my way into housing for the homeless until almost a decade after he died, but I wished Dad could walk through Moore Place and touch the walls that his confidence helped me build. I would have loved if he could stand in HopeWay and see it as the place we wanted to find for my mom. Dad had a faith in me that I did not find in myself until long after he was gone.

However odd it was to have a virtual stranger like Meg tell me she believed my dad knew all of that—well, it mattered more to me than she could ever know. Still, after receiving her message, I felt there were so many mysteries unsolved.

How did my book that began as a whisper to *Write it down* make its way to Buffalo? How did Meg's aunt Mary happen to find it on a windowsill and decide she must send it to her niece? Why did Meg feel that she "strongly and fiercely" received a message from my dad, a man twenty years dead whom she did not know?

I can't explain any of that. But I know that the message Meg received was exactly what I had long wanted to hear from my dad. Some might say that anyone could have known that those encouraging words would be meaningful. Of course, a daughter who has lost her father wishes he knew what she had done with her life and was proud of her. But of all the people who read my book, no one else has ever told me they received a message from my father for me about my words.

* * * *

Meg still receives and delivers messages to others because she has learned to see it as almost a sacred responsibility. She once had a friend who also received messages ask her, "So, are you going to let your ego stand in the way of delivering a message to someone who really needs it?"

She realized her friend was right. Meg had been more concerned about what others might think than the holiness of the task. Once she began to see how profoundly those messages mattered to people, she stopped worrying and just paid attention to what she received. "When I am walking in the woods or doing yoga, that's when I get them the most," she told me. "If I am super busy, I can't listen well."

Meg has learned to become comfortable hearing messages that used to make her uncomfortable. She also believes we are all capable of receiving such signs and messages if we are open to the idea. In Celtic spirituality, the still places where we can receive such messages are known as "thin places" where heaven and earth meet. There are some famous thin places people travel to, like the tiny island community of Iona off of Scotland, or along the five-hundred-kilometer Camino pilgrimage in Spain.[1] Others believe a thin place exists between the moments of life and death, and for Meg, these messages have changed how she views the end of her life.

"I think I have very little fear of passing away, other than leaving my family before I am ready," Meg said, tearing up as she said it. "It has made me believe we can still be with them." So many people are terrified of dying, but she finds that listening to these messages gives her hope. "If we can see death as transitioning to a different place where we can still love and be loved, it's less scary."

All I know for certain is that Meg and I, once strangers, are now the best of friends. Two peas in a pod who might never have met except for her aunt Mary and my dad who still loves me—and I can love him from a very thin place.

8

Miss Jo: Never Too Late

While it still remains a mystery how my book made it to Buffalo, the next God Dot, which popped up in Kingsport, Tennessee, was easier to explain. Liz Clasen-Kelly sent me another email—this time about a woman from her hometown who heard a whisper after reading my book. Liz shared the story in a late-night email:

> Just a fun story to pass along to you tonight. In my hometown there is an amazing woman named Jo Morrison. . . . My mother (proud mother that she is) passed along your book to her. She has decided that the Spirit has called her to work on homelessness in the time she has left. She has [also] passed the book along to her circle of support, and they are prayerfully considering what to do. I think she will come visit Moore Place. That story made my night. Love to watch the Holy Spirit at work.

That story made my night as well, and I wanted to find out more about "Miss Jo," as she was affectionately known in Kingsport. Long before she read my book, Miss Jo had been Liz's youth group leader at church and an active volunteer in housing efforts. In 1985, a friend had asked Miss Jo to help start a Habitat for Humanity affiliate in Eastern Tennessee.

"My husband had just passed away and I had time, so I did!" Miss Jo told me later.

Eventually, that affiliate would house over three hundred families. In 1996, the governor heard about Miss Jo and recruited her for a new statewide housing initiative. "The governor was stomping the streets to win an election, and people asked him to do something about affordable housing," she recalled.

It became known as the Affordable Housing Task Force in Tennessee, and after working on the state effort, Miss Jo created a local program in Kingsport as well. She gathered developers and bankers to work together for families who couldn't afford housing or who didn't know how to negotiate a loan in Kingsport. "So that was another ten-year project," Miss Jo said, and laughed.

By the time Miss Jo got a copy of my book, she already understood the power of creating housing for families. But the idea of permanent supportive housing for the homeless, like Moore Place, was new to her. After reading about it, she started to hear a whisper that she needed to do more—she needed to help build something for the homeless in Kingsport.

And here's the truly remarkable part of her story. When Miss Jo read *The Hundred Story Home*, she was one hundred years old!

The fact that she was a very senior citizen might have deterred some people, but Miss Jo did not believe her age meant she was too old to begin anything. She explained to me that while *The Hundred Story Home* helped her whisper begin, it took a different kind of epiphany for Miss Jo to decide to listen. She was coming back from church one night, and there was a terrible storm.

"It was a wintry night in late February," she said. "My friend Betsy was driving. It was pouring down rain and dark and gloomy."

Miss Jo doesn't remember what the church program was about that night, but she is positive it was not about homelessness. That is an important part of her story, because it makes what happened next all the more unusual to her.

"We were pulling out of the parking lot, and all of a sudden it was one of those winter electrical storms," she said. "There was a streak of lightning and out of my mouth came, 'Oh Betsy, where do you think the homeless are sleeping tonight?'"

It was a strange thought to pop into Miss Jo's head. Even years later, she would remember only that she could not shake the idea that on a night like this, there were homeless men and women in Kingsport huddled under trees and makeshift shelters with no place to escape the storm.

That night, she felt her whisper become a shout that she must *Do something about it.*

While many people who are only seventy or even eighty years old might think it is "too late" to try something new, centenarian Miss Jo was just getting started. She began talking with influential people in Kingsport about her idea. After some time, she persuaded local leaders to travel to Charlotte to see Moore Place in person. Liz helped arrange a field trip for the group of twenty so they could see what might be possible in Kingsport.

That morning, Liz and I waited at Moore Place to greet Miss Jo and the two vanfuls of people with her. As they unloaded, Miss Jo was easy to recognize. She had soft white curls, large round glasses, and a bright red sweater.

"Oh, I wouldn't have missed this for anything!" she said, giving me a huge hug.

When she gave me that hug, Miss Jo was 102 years old. She moved slowly toward the doors of Moore Place, pushing her walker, but despite her deliberate pace, she was as excited as a teenager. As Liz and I gave the group a tour, Miss Jo peppered us with questions. Seeing Moore Place in person that day, she was even more convinced than she had been on the night she was struck with the idea as if by lightning.

Miss Jo told us her visit to Charlotte was "A shot in the arm!" She returned to Tennessee and formed a new nonprofit called the Kingsport Homeless Ministry. As she turned 103, she served on the board and helped lead a search for a property where they could build a shelter for those experiencing homelessness.

A year later, as the COVID pandemic took over the world, I checked on Miss Jo because I was worried that the virus might've threatened her health or dampened her spirits. In 1918, Miss Jo's father had died from the Spanish flu epidemic, and three years later, her mother had died from health complications attributed to the same illness. Miss Jo, however, was safe from COVID and answered my email right away.

She wrote that while they were having difficulties with zoning, she and her dream of building housing were both very much alive and well. Kingsport business owners were complaining that something needed to be done about "homeless people sleeping in their doorways," yet those same business owners fought Miss Jo's attempts to buy property on which to build housing to get people off the streets and out of those same doorways.

Her email ended with,

> Just celebrated my 104th birthday! Eyesight failing and on a walker. Blessed with a lot of help. Will try to keep you posted. Love, Jo Morrison

What other 104-year-old woman with failing eyesight would even attempt a huge building project? I told her that in a Zoom call we arranged later that year. "Miss Jo, I talk to a lot of women who at even fifty-four years old think it is too late to accomplish something or dream a new dream for their lives!"

Miss Jo laughed. "I guess I could have just stayed at home in my rocking chair," she told me. "But life is so much richer when you become involved with some worthwhile cause outside yourself."

We talked for almost an hour that day, and she ended our call with these words: "Each day is a gift. If you get up in the morning, pray that God will show you what he wants you to do. That's the only advice I have. Keep listening."

9

Jackie: A Lamp and a Toaster

Listening seemed to be the one constant in all the God Dot connections I was discovering, whether it was paying attention to my own whispers, hearing about others like Caroline Bundy, or marveling at Miss Jo's late-in-life whisper and wisdom. But even though I was trying to pay attention, I almost missed the next God Dot waiting to be discovered in my inbox.

The email was from a woman named Jackie Craig:

> Hi, Kathy—I would like to see if you might be interested/available when you're in Raleigh. You see, I've been reading your book over the past few days and feel such a kinship to your story and the God-sized dream that resulted! I am currently the executive director at The Green Chair Project in Raleigh, a nonprofit that equips homes with essential furnishings for individuals in need as they recover from homelessness, crisis, and disaster . . . all with tremendous dignity. And that's where I think our interests, passions, and journeys are very similar.

When I read Jackie's email, I thought she was someone I had met several months earlier. Both organizations had "Green" in their name, and both were nonprofits providing furniture assistance. I immediately responded yes to Jackie's invitation, though it turned out I actually had no idea who I was about to meet.

When I turned into the parking lot that my GPS assured me was the correct address, I immediately thought I was at the wrong door. Expecting a small nonprofit operating out of a church, I had arrived instead at a huge warehouse with bright green wooden chairs scattered throughout its front lawn. A hand-painted, whimsical sign greeted me:

The Green Chair Project
Welcomes
All Colors | All Sizes
All Ages | All Countries
All Genders | All Types
All Cultures | All Beliefs
ALL
PEOPLE
SAFE PLACE

As I was studying this message, another car pulled up, and its driver waved to me. As she got out of her car, I could see that she had shoulder-length silver hair, stylish hoop earrings, and a long, tassel necklace over her pink sweater.

"So great to finally meet you!" Jackie Craig said.

"I know!" I said, not yet willing to admit I had no idea who she was or why I was there.

"Come in," Jackie said as she unlocked the double glass doors.

As I followed her inside, I was immediately impressed by the space. I had been in ministry warehouses before, but none of them looked as nice as this. Jackie's place was not a collection of ragged cast-off couches. This was like entering a vintage boutique store.

The display at the front had an orange velvet sofa artfully arranged with blue patterned pillows. Alongside were matching cobalt blue chairs, a cream coffee table stacked with home design magazines, and a bowl of bright green apples. This scene was set in front of an ivory wooden mantel that held oversize decorative letters spelling out the word HOME. Painted on the mantel in script was the mission of Green Chair: "Reusing Furniture. Renewing Lives."

Looking around the giant space, I could see that past this opening collection were dozens of similar groupings, each as artfully styled. Everything had been cleaned and curated, and some items were brightly painted, giving the pieces a completely new look. Jackie smiled, watching me take it all in.

"This is a furniture ministry, not a store, right?" I clarified, making sure I had not misinterpreted Jackie's original email.

She nodded with pride. "Yes, clients 'shop' to find the furniture they like for their own home, and they also pay a small fee that provides the dignity of ownership. Families are referred by social service agencies, and then they make appointments to come and choose their furniture."

Jackie began giving me a grand tour of Green Chair. The space was divided by types of furniture, just like a commercial store: dining room, living room, and bedroom. There were also displays for linens and dishes, along with accent pillows and accessories. Behind the displays were giant workspaces where the volunteers made the magic happen. Donated items might arrive slightly battered, but the volunteers gave everything new life. Dishes were cleaned, linens were pressed, and even draperies were cut into new, more useable curtains. The scale of the building and the mission was beyond impressive, but even more than that, it was love that shone through.

Something had been nudging me the whole time Jackie was talking. I remembered how I had heard *Ask her what she does* when I was on the plane beside Beverly Burnett, and she turned out to be a speaker. As I looked around this amazing ministry, I was hearing a slightly different whisper: *Ask her why she did it.*

There had to be a story. I did not know her, but I was willing to bet all of this began with a whisper, like it had for Caroline Bundy and Miss Jo. One that felt inconvenient, unexpected, and uncomfortable.

"Jackie," I interrupted. "I have to know. Why did you start this? How did you know you were meant to do this?"

Jackie grew quiet and smiled at me. We locked eyes, and I knew by the tears welling up she knew exactly what I was talking about. "It was all God's idea, and we are just trying to keep up!" she said. I opened my notebook and began to scribble notes as fast as I could to keep up with her story.

· · · ·

Growing up, Jackie was an only child. She remembered playing alone for hours with a pretend cash register and imaginary customers in her play store.

"I guess I was always in sales." She laughed. "It was my thing."

Jackie met her husband, Lee, while they were in college at Ball State University in Muncie, Indiana. Upon graduation, she began her career in sales at a check printing company. Her career brought her to Raleigh while Lee, an economics professor, joined the faculty at North Carolina State University. They raised their two daughters in Raleigh. Jackie never thought she would be a stay-at-home mom, but in order for Lee to be able to travel for his job, she eventually gave up her paid work in sales and marketing. Ever the achiever, she took lead volunteer roles, like president of the PTA and organizer for Bible studies.

One Christmas, she was in charge of a unique project for her church. Jackie was going to hang large portraits of people experiencing homelessness in the sanctuary windows. Along with the photography installations were banners that read "What Are You Waiting For?" These larger-than-life faces seemed to be pleading for help.

As she climbed up and down the ladder with the portraits, Jackie wrestled with God and with herself. *What can I do?* she thought. *What am I waiting for?* She felt there was some purpose she was meant to find, but like me, she couldn't see any neon sign pointing her in the right direction.

A few years before, Jackie had started volunteering for a women's prison ministry, leading art projects. While the women worked on their crafts, Jackie would hear their stories. Life was difficult not only in prison but sometimes even more so when they got out. Setting up a new life in an apartment with no savings and only the money from a minimum wage job was a challenging endeavor. Then, when her mother-in-law died, Jackie had to sort through many household items, and it made her think of one of the women who would soon be getting out of prison.

"As we wondered what to do with everything, I thought about how she could use my mother-in-law's TV because she didn't have anything," she told me. The gift was meant to be a one-time act of kindness, but Jackie remembered how it made her feel. "I love stuff, but it is easy to part with stuff if you know someone else needs it."

That memory of giving that woman something to help her in her new life and the Christmas photography exhibit began haunting Jackie. She kept remembering those words: *What are you waiting for?*

"I had this feeling I was supposed to be doing something with furniture and this prison ministry or the homeless, but I couldn't quite see it yet," she said.

Although Jackie's whisper felt very vague, it was also very insistent. One day, as she was getting dressed for her Bible study group, she decided she'd had enough. She said out loud, "God, whatever this is, either get it out of my head or let's get on with it."

As she walked into the church building for her study, a woman in her group approached her. "Jackie, do you know anyone who could use a toaster?" Jackie could barely reply before the woman added, "And I have a lamp in the car if you can use that too."

It was a moment like Miss Jo's lightning storm epiphany. She was completely thunderstruck, and everything began to come together.

Why, yes. Yes, she did know someone.

Jackie was acquainted with another woman who was getting out of prison and could certainly use that toaster and that lamp. At that moment, while she was standing in the church hallway, Green Chair was born.

"God uses everything we do," she told me. "Every experience we've had and everyone we know to come alongside."

Along with another Bible study member, Jackie started by letting her congregation know that if there were items they didn't need, she knew women who did. They borrowed a closet in the church building, and it soon filled up as others began donating gently used items for people who needed them. The closet soon overflowed into a Sunday school room, and then finally into an office furniture warehouse donated by a businessperson with a huge heart. The abundance was overwhelming, but so was the need. Jackie matched families with furniture and volunteers with purpose.

To this day, the beauty of Jackie's mission stretches far beyond the thrift store model. Everything in Green Chair is infused with love and choice. Families coming out of homelessness are not forced to take something just because they have nothing. They are offered the ability to freely choose what they need to make their apartments feel like home. Everything from dish sets to couches are available for them to start fresh. A life of new beginnings, where items once loved can be loved again. A life of dignity, and, for Jackie, a life of destiny.

On her office shelf is a fading photo of her seated beside her father, who is wearing a blue pullover and red tie. Six-year-old Jackie wears an orange patterned dress and white tights and has a pixie haircut. In the photo, she is opening a birthday present of Barbie-sized furniture. Next to the photo, Jackie still has some of the remaining pieces of that same furniture set. To her, these tiny pieces are small reminders of God's patience.

"Maybe I always knew what I would be doing." Jackie smiled. Somewhere between the women's prison ministry and the lamp and the toaster, she finally understood and listened to her whisper. She was almost forty-five years old, but Jackie knew it was exactly what she had been waiting for.

Trusting that faint, vague whisper strengthened her faith about her own life. "In all these years, we have never been unable to provide a couch for a family or a bed for a child," she said. "If God can do that, I can trust him in my own life with every detail."

If we keep our heads down and stop listening for God, we miss the connections with grace, and we miss becoming who we were meant to be. Jackie admits it can be scary to trust a whisper but considers it like a muscle to be exercised.

"Women especially have so many seasons in our lives, and one leads to another, but why are we so hesitant to believe that?" she asked. "We want everything spelled out, and we want proof something will work before we make a change. But that's not faith, that's fact."

In her own life, Jackie has learned to listen and trust, especially when she is uncertain where a whisper might be leading her. On the shelf beside the childhood photo and doll furniture, she reminds herself of this with a sign that reads, "A leap of faith never fails."

10

Lesley: "Yellow Pants" Whisper

After what felt like another meant-to-be meeting, with Jackie, I was beginning to look at life differently. All the remarkable women I was encountering, such as Beverly Burnett, Frances Hailey, and Miss Jo, had me wondering about how the world really worked. Each story felt like a shimmering pearl all by itself, but when strung together, these connections were starting to add up to evidence of something much bigger.

The whispers I'd heard and followed seemed to be a common thread for so many other stories as well. Betsy Blue following a whisper to HopeWay. Caroline Bundy following a whisper to the Way Station. Jackie Craig following a whisper to Green Chair. Maybe these whispers were like a built-in compass, leading us to our true-life paths. At the same time, I wasn't clear how to interpret this little inner voice. Was it God speaking so clearly to us that it felt as if he was talking from somewhere deep in our souls? Or was it just our souls, aching to be heard? If those whispers were God, then surely he was not just whispering to a few people. He must be speaking directly to each of us, yet he was whispering in a world that had become too loud in which to be heard.

I found a different and deeper explanation buried in the pages of a novel. In *Rare Objects*, author Kathleen Tessaro crafts a world of intrigue about antique shops for her main character, Maeve. The story is historical fiction set in Depression-era Boston, and I was reading it for entertainment, not enlightenment. But just like Maeve, who discovered treasures in rare antiques, I found this beautiful image:

> There is a word in Hebrew—*nitzotzot*. It means "divine sparks." It refers to the infinitesimal fragments of godliness that inhabit everything—all of creation, both animate and inanimate. When something is used as it was divinely intended, these sparks are said to be "liberated"; they shine, become a reflection of the face of God himself in this transient world.[1]

I read that passage over and over. Through further research, I learned this Hebrew word *nitzotzot* is plural, not singular. The idea of these sparks within each of us that connect us to God and to our greater purpose made so much sense to me. While there are many interpretive stories about *nitzotzot*, one of the most common is the idea that each of us are "sparks of light." Early Jewish mystics believed in the idea that the world was a vessel that broke apart, and our task in life was to repair the world by bringing all the sparks back together. This idea is known as *tikkun olam*, which translates to "mend the world" or "heal the world."[2] Many modern-day American Jews believe this is a central teaching for life, and our purpose is to help repair what is broken in society.

I began to think that this mending was what these God Dot connections were about. Not how each of us can do anything as individuals but how together we can plug into God's "divine electricity" to shine our light and repair our world.

While I continued to speak to groups about *The Hundred Story Home*, I started to see those events were less about talking and more about listening. They were about finding people who already knew they were hearing a whisper. Who were the other Caroline Bundys with an idea that might repair the world? Maybe my purpose in life now was as simple as encouraging people to listen and bearing witness to what they did with their light.

. . . .

One night, at a church talk in Charlotte, something very unusual happened. As I was speaking, my eyes were drawn to one particular woman in the crowd. It was as if there was a light around her that made her glow and stand out from the other people in the room. Her face was blocked by others sitting in front of her, but I could see she was wearing a white shirt and yellow pants. I didn't get a good look at the pants until she stood afterward, but those pants were so distinctively yellow, like butter.

I remember thinking, *It's her. I am supposed to be talking to her.*

Whoever she was, I wanted to be certain we met, so I encouraged the audience to talk with me after the program if they had a whisper. "I like to help people listen to what is calling them," I told the group.

As I was signing books, I could see that "yellow pants" was waiting in line. I also noticed she had short brown hair, but I still did not get a good look at her face because of the crowd. While I genuinely listened to each person as I signed their book, I was just waiting for "yellow pants." I just knew in my soul she had a story I needed to hear.

The line kept inching forward until there were just a few people before her turn. The next woman in line, however, started telling me a very long but dear story. By the time she had finished, "yellow pants" had disappeared.

I finished the signing and packed up slowly, hoping she might return, but the mystery woman was gone. Maybe she had grown impatient or lost her nerve. Whatever her reasons, I had missed the opportunity to know what she wanted to say. Even though I'd heard many lovely and powerful stories that night, I felt oddly crushed.

I just knew I was supposed to talk with her. I was certain. How would I ever find her?

"There was a woman here tonight," I said to the remaining church members as we all gathered to leave the fellowship hall. "She had brown hair, a white shirt, and yellow pants." But no one seemed to know who I was talking about. Apparently, she had been glowing only to me.

I had trouble falling asleep that night, wondering what I had missed. What whisper was she hearing and how was I supposed to help her listen? The next morning, I woke up to see I'd received an email from a woman named Lesley Faulkner:

> Hi Kathy! I heard you speak last night but didn't get a chance to say "thank you" before I had to leave. Thank you!!!
>
> I was invited to a True Blessings luncheon about seven years ago. I had the honor of sitting with Liz Clasen-Kelly. She told me in detail about Roof Above and Moore Place; her passion for these two places and our neighbors was evident. Although it took me two years to volunteer, I finally listened to that whisper! I now volunteer every Friday at the Roof Above help desk. I have been there about five years and just love it! I also volunteer at Moore Place three Mondays a month. My two friends and I run the art program, which actually is more crafts . . . and coffee.

Lesley went on to say she was listening to another whisper but just "needed to figure out where it is leading me." I reread the email, getting a little more excited. Was it her? Was this email from "yellow pants"?

I wrote back:

Dear Lesley,

Thank you so much for this great email. Weird question—were you wearing yellow jeans and a white top last night? I saw a woman waiting to speak with me but never got to talk to her. Hoping this is you because I wanted to connect with that woman—if it was not you, thank you for this great message! So love that you are a volunteer and connect through Liz Clasen-Kelly, one of the world's best people. If you would like to get together and have coffee to discuss whispers, I would love to! I truly feel that is a part of this next chapter for me.

Lesley's answer arrived late in the day:

Yes, that was me.

When I read that, I felt that full-body tingle, like physical proof of our God Dot connection. I had found her. Just like with Caroline Bundy, I knew I was supposed to hear Lesley's whisper and encourage her.

It took a few weeks for our calendars to align, but we finally met for coffee. As we sat across from each other, I could see she was probably in her forties, with brown eyes and creamy skin. When Lesley smiled, it was an invitation to smile with her—welcoming and full.

Lesley was married to a civil engineer, David, whom she said at one time had "built bridges but now built neighborhoods." Because of his job, David and Lesley had moved around a lot in their early marriage—five times in four years.

"Wasn't that hard? All the moving?" I asked.

Lesley nodded but then added, "But I love moving furniture."

"What? No one likes moving furniture!" I said.

"We all do it in my family." Lesley laughed. "My grandmother would come to visit and move our furniture around—it drove my dad crazy. My mom does it too, because she says it gives her a different outlook. If my mom doesn't have a new way to arrange the furniture, she moves the art. She even keeps a whole closet full of paintings and prints to change out for the seasons."

After all the moving, Lesley and David settled in Charlotte, where their two children, a son and a daughter, were born. Ever since college, Lesley had worked a series of jobs, and she loved working in customer service. She didn't have much experience volunteering outside her kids' school and church before the True Blessings luncheon where she sat next to Liz.

"She was just so passionate about her work and the people," Lesley remembered. "I guess I couldn't forget it."

By that time, she had worked part-time for almost seven years at a furniture consignment store and also had her real estate license. While real estate helped fill her need to help others, she also believed there was another purpose for her life she was missing. Something began whispering to Lesley—maybe it was a combination of volunteering at Moore Place, watching people move from homelessness to housing, and her part-time job at the consignment store watching furniture pieces get a new life.

She couldn't quite name or explain what it was that she was hearing. Finally, she asked me, "Have you ever heard of Jackie Craig and The Green Chair Project in Raleigh?"

Why, yes. Yes, I had.

It was truly amazing. A year before, I would not have known who or what she was talking about. After my accidental appointment with Jackie only a few months before, I knew exactly who Lesley meant and what was so special about Green Chair. Even more than that, I knew all about Jackie and the whisper that led her to create her incredible furniture nonprofit ministry.

That day, sitting across from Lesley having coffee, it felt like the reason I knew all about Jackie's whisper was so that I could encourage Lesley in her own.

"You need to go meet her," I told her. "Jackie is amazing, and you can't believe what her place is like!"

Within the month, Lesley made the road trip to Raleigh to see for herself. She came back from that trip both impressed and overwhelmed.

"It felt too big for me," Lesley told me after her visit. "When I saw that warehouse and the whole operation, it was just too big for me to think about doing."

Strangely, I was disappointed, because I'd started having my *own* whisper about Lesley's whisper. My whisper told me to keep telling her to listen. I felt this was exactly what she should be doing, even if she didn't have that same faith in herself.

Jackie had tried to tell Lesley that as well.

"Just do one," Jackie had encouraged her. "You don't have to start a whole nonprofit; you can just help one family."

Lesley wasn't sure how to do that either, but later that year she began volunteering for an outreach program at her kids' high school. "There were one hundred kids who were experiencing homelessness in our school, and only one social worker to help them all!" she told me.

That social worker mentioned to Lesley that one of those homeless families needed furniture. It reminded her of Jackie's advice: "Just do one."

So, Lesley did.

That year, she and some friends helped not just one but three families who needed furniture. "We were just a whole bunch of moms moving furniture!" Lesley laughed.

At the time, she did not know her whisper was just getting started and was going to get much, much louder. Her whisper was going to lead to something she could not have imagined for herself. Even though Lesley did not want to believe she was capable, her whisper was not going to let her go.

11

Priscilla: The Next Forty Years

As I kept connecting the God Dots in my life, I stopped being surprised by the connections and started being more expectant. In fact, if a week went by without discovering a remarkable story, I would wonder if I'd missed something. I came to believe that whispers and God Dots were all around us every day; we just had to be attuned and pay attention. With so many remarkable connections, I also began to believe there was nothing random or coincidental about them. They had to be a pattern of everyday grace.

A few months after I met with my new "yellow pants" friend, Lesley Faulkner, her whisper became another God Dot connection. A friend wrote me to ask if I would meet with a woman named Priscilla Chapman. She had read *The Hundred Story Home* and wanted to talk with me about it. My friend apologized, saying he was not quite sure why she wanted to meet me, but I was willing to bet Priscilla was another woman with a whisper.

When we met for coffee, she seemed a little unsure of where to start. Our high-top table was near a window, and we perched on stools facing each other. The sun lit the side of her face, making her dark brown hair shine. Priscilla and I were about the same height—five feet and not much more—so I wondered if, like me, her feet were barely reaching the crossbar. Priscilla was at least fifteen years younger than me, and I quickly learned she shared the same restlessness for purpose I had experienced ten years ago.

"When I read your book, I underlined the parts where you wrote about wondering what you were going to do with your life," she said.

Priscilla was a married mom with three children who were all growing up, so she was beginning to think about her own life again. In *The Hundred Story Home*, I had written about searching for my "forty-year thing," meaning that once you raise your children or launch a career (or both), then you sometimes have about forty years left to do something with your own life.

This idea had struck a chord with Priscilla, because she had just turned forty when she was reading the book. Although she had never done anything like it before, she had signed up for a yoga retreat because it felt right to celebrate her fourth decade with self-care and reflection.

She told me that while at the retreat, she was in the yoga child's pose when the thought hit her, *I am forty years old, and I have forty years left. I have absolutely no idea what to do with my life.* Looking back, she knew this was the moment her whisper began telling her to *Do something*, but she had no idea what that meant. Priscilla only knew that her life had become far too small.

"All I worried about were my kids and what I was going to wear," she said. "I just knew I had to do more on this earth than worry about what I was going to wear!" She had grown up in the small town of Versailles, Kentucky, with a population of seven thousand, and was part of a blended family of four children: a half brother, a half sister, Priscilla, and her younger brother. Both of her brothers had struggled with addiction, especially her younger brother.

"Our family had to practice a lot of tough love," she said. "My brother sometimes lived in halfway homes, so I think that is another reason I connected with your book."

Priscilla remembered visiting her brother in a halfway house as well as receiving some desperate collect phone calls. "Our family was seen as a successful family in our small town, yet that is what was really happening," she said, shaking her head. "You just never know what is happening in some people's lives."

She wasn't sure what to do with her whisper to do something more with her life, but one day her daughter, Ellen, came home from school talking about a presentation from a visiting author. As it turned out, I had spoken that day to Ellen's fourth-grade class about my children's book *A Good Night for Mr. Coleman*.

"Mom, that lady whose book you liked talked at school today," Ellen said.

She could not figure out who Ellen was talking about. The only local author she knew of wrote racy adult fiction, so why would the school have that writer talking to fourth graders?

"No," Ellen said. "The lady who wrote the homeless book."

Priscilla couldn't even remember mentioning *The Hundred Story Home* to her youngest daughter, but she must have. "She told us about the power of one person and how even a kid can make a difference," her daughter said. "There's a boy who made blessing bags and gave them to people on the streets. I want to do that."

Ellen was talking about Jahkil Naeem Jackson, a boy in Chicago who listened to a whisper to do something for those in need when he was only eight years old. After helping his aunt distribute food to the homeless, he knew he wanted to do more. His whisper was to create what he called "Blessing Bags." He filled small bags with socks, deodorant, granola bars, toothbrushes, toothpaste, bottled water, and more. Whenever I talked with school children about homelessness, I used Jahkil as an example of how small ideas can make a big difference. His desire to do good launched a nonprofit,

Project I Am, that has touched tens of thousands of people and inspired others to do the same.[1]

That Christmas, before I met Priscilla, she and Ellen created their own Blessing Bags and distributed them around Charlotte. This mother-daughter service project is what led Priscilla to tell our mutual friend she would like to meet me. When her friend actually arranged our meeting through email, Priscilla thought, *Oh, no! Now I have to show up! What am I going to say?*

She smiled while telling me this. "I loved the idea from your book to 'trust the whisper,'" she added. "But I don't know that I have heard mine. I keep waiting for that idea that won't go away."

We talked about a lot of ideas as I tried to listen for her specific whisper. When having these "whisper" coffees, I was learning to ask people a specific question: What breaks your heart? I had come to believe there is something imprinted on each person's heart unique to them.

It is our individual experiences that shape us, so what matters deeply to one person will not be the same for another. And usually, somewhere in their answer is a clue to that person's calling.

As we discussed different nonprofits in Charlotte, Priscilla looked interested, but she didn't light up until we started talking about Jackie Craig's The Green Chair Project. Her already huge, round eyes grew wider as I explained the idea of Jackie's furniture ministry. "What's so special about it is the choice they give people," I said. "So often people are just made to take whatever is donated. But Green Chair makes it this incredibly dignified shopping experience to make a house a home."

Ever since I had met Jackie a year before, I had tried to convince her to bring Green Chair to Charlotte, but she was not hearing that whisper. Seeing Priscilla's enthusiasm, I remembered how excited Lesley Faulkner, my "yellow pants" friend, was about the idea but had felt it was too big for her to start alone.

Although I did not believe the Green Chair idea was my whisper to follow, there was something about it that would not let me go. Maybe I was just supposed to help the people who were meant to create it. I could think of at least ten women I had talked with recently who wanted to do something they couldn't quite name. What if I helped all those women connect to see what happened?

Three weeks after Priscilla and I had coffee, over a dozen women gathered with me around a table to talk about starting a program like The Green Chair Project in Charlotte, including Lesley Faulkner, Priscilla Chapman, and another longtime friend of mine named Mary Beth Hollett. As everybody chose a chair, Lesley, Priscilla, and Mary Beth happened to sit together even though none of them knew each other.

After we discussed the idea, I decided to go around the table to gauge everyone's level of interest. I asked each person to say whether they might be a project leader or simply a helper. One by one, everyone at the table said they were very interested in the idea but declared themselves to be helpers. No one wanted to lead the charge.

As we adjourned the meeting, I was deflated. I had been certain someone was going to hear their whisper loud and clear, but apparently it all just felt too big. Then, as everyone was leaving, I saw Lesley, Priscilla, and Mary Beth still talking. Something nudged me to say to them, "Maybe none of you think you are leaders, but I do! I think the three of you should keep meeting."

They agreed, and started meeting to see what might be possible. They even planned a road trip to Raleigh to visit Green Chair and meet Jackie Craig in person. "I was so overwhelmed, seeing what it could be," Priscilla said. "They were ten years ahead of us, and I just remember thinking we had so much work to do."

The first couple of times Lesley, Priscilla, and Mary Beth met, it seemed like nothing was moving because there were so many hurdles in the way. "I was worried about the legal implications," Mary Beth said. "We needed to create a nonprofit with articles of incorporation. I didn't know how to do that."

"The donation part was what concerned me," Priscilla said. "If we promised furnishings, where would we get them? What if we ran out?"

"I didn't know if agencies would want to work with us," admitted Lesley. "At one of our very first community meetings, some guy told us we would only ever be 'women with a hobby.'"

But that guy couldn't have been more wrong. It took only six months to create their nonprofit, Furnish for Good. "The real magic happened when we brainstormed and just went for it," Mary Beth said. "The word *no* never got in our way, and that's when we realized that Furnish for Good could be whatever we wanted it to be. We *believed* we could make anything happen, and we did it."

Together, Lesley, Priscilla, and Mary Beth created a website, found 4,000 square feet of office space, and began serving families. Like Green Chair, Furnish for Good was set up to allow each family or individual moving out of homelessness to choose their furnishings from a selection of items that had been cleaned, curated, and made ready for a new home.

After all the start-up work, they began to see the true impact they were making when they helped people move home for the first time. "When you see our families with the joy and pride of sitting on their new sofas, it is *real*," Priscilla said. "It is real emotion."

Even through the disruptive pandemic years, Lesley, Priscilla, Mary Beth, and dozens of volunteers still moved in an average of four households a week, and each of the founders had a particular strength. Lesley managed donations, Priscilla handled the clients, and Mary Beth tackled the administrative needs. They came to love each other as much as the work.

"Lesley can find anything," Mary Beth said with a laugh, while Lesley credited Priscilla. "She is our fearless leader! She sets up every appointment for our clients. She works with all our partner agencies and the social workers to choose furnishings. She is amazing!"

Priscilla, in turn, shrugged off the compliment. "It is just incredible how every time we have needed something, it just seemed to appear. We are about to run out of couches, for example, and then Lesley calls to say she found some!"

It is this type of miraculous abundance, and all the God Dot connections that have aligned, that changed the way Lesley sees the world. "All the moving pieces that had to come together to make this happen—it couldn't be coincidence! It has to be a higher power," she said.

In following her whisper to create Furnish for Good, Lesley felt her faith change, strengthening her belief not only in God but in other people as well. "For all the people we help, and what they have gone through in their lives, I see how so many have relied on faith to get through," she told me. "I used to panic about whether we would have enough donations to pay our warehouse rent or enough dressers for everyone. Now I just remind myself to have faith it will all happen. I trust it will happen."

Lesley gave up her real estate career to work full-time at Furnish for Good, and that changed her perspective as well. "Working in real estate, I thought gentrification was good because it meant higher sale prices. From this side of the table, I see it through a very different lens. Now I hear stories from our families that show me how gentrification can push people out of their homes."

What once felt like a whisper too big to follow now feels like what Lesley was born to do. "It is still big, but it feels doable—and there is still so much more to do!" she said.

As many families as they have helped, the phone still rings with more, but she doesn't get overwhelmed. With Priscilla, Mary Beth, and all the volunteers and donors by her side, Lesley no longer feels as if she is on an island by herself.

"It's not just my whisper anymore," she said. "It's everyone's!"

Now in their fourth year, Furnish for Good has hired their first official executive director, who will be leading their nonprofit into the future. Priscilla has a new whisper calling her to her next chapter, and she believes that learning to listen has created a lasting effect on her life and faith. "After listening to the first whisper, it's impossible to silence that for the rest of my life!" she said.

Mary Beth feels that listening to her whisper to help create Furnish for Good has changed her life for the better as well. "Priscilla and Lesley have made me a better human being. They've taught me how to love better, how to do better," she said. "We didn't know each other before we started brainstorming about Furnish for Good, but we knew we wanted to tap into something. Just listening to that quiet nudge has pushed me into a richer, deeper life."

It's difficult to say who first heard the whisper that began Furnish for Good, but Mary Beth puts it this way: "Collectively, we each were looking for more. Collectively, we cheered each other on. And collectively, we answered with a yes."

12

Lucy: The Lost Twin

The divine string of beads that began with Jackie Craig and led to Lesley, Priscilla, and Mary Beth was the first series of connected whispers that made me believe truly anything can happen in this God Dot world. Meeting Lucy Fields would begin a second series of connections that still leaves me shaking my head in wonder at it all.

Lucy and I were introduced at a monthly women's group called Moderate Chic, which invited speakers to come and present on a range of topics from politics to community matters. The evening I met Lucy, about forty women filled the living room and adjoining kitchen of a member's home to hear me speak about *The Hundred Story Home* and homelessness.

Lucy Fields happened to sit in an armchair directly in front of me, but I am not sure I noticed her even though she was only a few feet away. Standing before the women, I tried to look calm, but in truth, I still got nervous. No matter the size of the group, I always made meticulous notes for a presentation. Sometimes I even wrote, "Hi, I'm Kathy Izard" at the top of the page in case I had a complete blank and needed to remember who I was and why I came.

These women were easy to talk with, however, and seemed to be following and understanding my major points. When I talked about looking for purpose in my life, many nodded along. When I admitted I used to believe homelessness was an unsolvable problem, the women seemed to agree that is what they thought too.

Just as I was beginning to describe how Denver had asked me the four questions that changed my life, Lucy suddenly stood up right in front of me. She was a good five inches taller than me, so I had to look up to see her face. Her eyes were filled with tears, and she looked genuinely distraught.

"I am sorry," she said, looking me straight in the eye before ducking her head and rushing from the room.

Everyone was silent, and I tried to collect my thoughts. What could I have said that upset her so deeply? Typically, it was later in my talk that I could see people get emotional. There were a few stories that seemed to bring a tear—but not this early in my presentation. I found my place in my notes and continued on script, but Lucy's empty chair haunted me a bit. After we finished, I decided, I would need to find her to understand what happened.

I didn't need to wait until the end, however, because a few minutes later, Lucy came back into the room. Her shiny dark hair was pulled back from her forehead and fell in thick waves past her shoulders. Her face was slightly red from crying, but she looked more composed. She seemed to be waiting for a moment to quietly reclaim her seat without further interruption. I paused and stepped back a little so Lucy could sit back down in the armchair.

"I am sorry," she said again, but this time with more embarrassment than regret. "I think I am supposed to hear this."

She sat back down, and there was once again complete silence in the room. Lucy looked at me expectantly, waiting for me to continue. I have to admit I felt more than a little undone.

What had I said? What did she need to hear? Should I back up and repeat what she had missed? Or should I just move forward?

There was an awkward pause while I considered the options, and eventually I decided to pick up where I left off. As I spoke, Lucy paid full attention. Every once in a while, she would wipe a single tear from her cheek, but she stayed focused, her eyes letting me know that she was absorbing every word.

We wrapped up with questions from the group, and then I pulled Lucy aside for a private conversation. "Is there something we need to be talking about?" I asked her.

Lucy's expression tightened, and she nodded. "I am a twin, and I haven't seen my sister in years." She paused a moment before adding the truly surprising part of her story. "She is homeless, and I think it is time I found her."

My heart skipped a beat. I thought of my own twin daughters, Emma and Maddie, who had regularly alternated between being best friends and rivals. Now in their twenties, they had settled into a deep love for each other. I could not imagine what it would be like if they had not seen each other in years, much less if one truly became lost to the other.

"I am so sorry," I said, and felt that my words were completely inadequate.

Lucy and I agreed to connect again so that she could share the whole story, and we met a few days later. As she entered the bakery where we had agreed to meet for coffee, I was struck by Lucy's physical beauty. With her height and willowy frame, she looked elegant no matter what she wore. Lucy had worn a dress to the women's gathering, but even in jeans as she was that day, she was stunning. She had a light about her that made you look twice, as if she was a movie star you had seen before but whose name you could not recall. Lucy, however, seemed not to know this about herself. She draped easily into the wooden seat across from me, and we began talking.

There was so much to learn about her. Like my own family, she was one of three sisters, but in her case one older sibling, followed by fraternal twins Lucy and Ellie.

"Ellie's seven minutes older than me," she told me. "We were best friends and shared a room growing up. We were attached at the hip." She was an extrovert, while Ellie was an introvert. "Ellie was quiet in class, but she was very active in our high school. She was on the student council and had lots of friends." Lucy also described Ellie as a smart and diligent student who shined on the soccer field. "She was a great player. Ellie made the 4A all-conference women's team our senior year of high school—one of the top eleven players out of the most competitive high school conference in the state!"

Lucy and Ellie chose to go to UNC-Chapel Hill together, but for the first time in their lives, the sisters did not share a room. Although they were in the same dorm, they were on different floors. "It was in college when Ellie started to unravel," Lucy admitted, staring into her coffee. Her brown eyes filled with the same sorrow I had seen in the living room just days before.

"Ellie got worse and worse. I didn't know what was happening to her, and she couldn't explain it either," she said. "We were baffled. It was a lot for a couple of eighteen-year-olds to handle and try to figure out."

At the time, neither Lucy nor Ellie understood what was happening. As she described Ellie's behavior, I sensed that Lucy was going to tell me the eventual problem would be a mental health disorder—and it was. Just like my mom and Dru Abram's son, Mitch, Ellie was diagnosed with bipolar disorder, and each year of college she fell a little deeper into the abyss.

"By our senior year, I was worried she wouldn't graduate," Lucy said. "But Ellie is very smart, so she was able to pull it together to get her degree."

Ellie did receive a BA in English literature, but she never found her footing after college. "During our twenties, Ellie moved around and tried different paths, but she was battling severe mental illness with no support and a lot of pressure from our parents to get her act together," Lucy said. "It was a recipe for disaster."

She tried to help Ellie many times but wasn't sure what her sister needed. At the same time, Lucy was building her own life. She finished graduate school and began her career in Charlotte. Over time, Lucy married her husband, Greg, and they had two children, Jacob and Ally.

"I was living my life but at the same time feeling this hole. Ellie was falling apart, and I couldn't do anything to help her," she said, tearing up. "Ellie stayed in the Raleigh area, and it was too far away for me to really make a difference in her life."

As we talked, Lucy turned from her twin's troubles to her own marriage, career, and family. As it turned out, her son, Jacob, needed much of her time and attention. While he'd had colic, Jacob was otherwise completely healthy until he was about ten months old. Then, almost overnight, he started becoming very difficult, with obsessive behavior, severe food and sensory issues, and intense fits of violent rage.

"He was my first child, so I didn't know any better, but it was almost as if he were possessed," Lucy said. "That began our ten-year search for answers."

Over the next decade, she would consult sixteen different doctors and specialists, including their pediatrician and multiple psychiatrists, psychologists, and neurologists. Jacob would have brief periods when his symptoms would wane, then months plagued by severe rage, violence, depression, anxiety, obsessive-compulsive behaviors, and constant suicidal ideation. Doctors suggested multiple diagnoses, including sensory processing disorder, anxiety, oppositional defiant disorder, and attention deficit hyperactivity disorder. But while some of these matched Jacob's symptoms, Lucy still believed there was a root cause they were missing.

She teared up again as she recounted her family's medical mystery and exhaustive search for the answer. It became all-consuming for Lucy, and she eventually discovered Jacob's diagnosis was a commonly missed and often misunderstood disease. "Have you ever heard of PANS?" she asked.

Although we had raised four daughters with numerous medical problems over the years, this was a new term for me. Lucy began to describe PANS—pediatric acute-onset neuropsychiatric syndrome—which is an autoimmune disease that affects the brain. It was only first recognized in 1998. Children with PANS experience a misdirected bodily response to an infection; their immune system attacks the brain, causing a wide variety of mental health symptoms.[1] She learned a diagnosis of PANS should be considered whenever symptoms of OCD, eating restrictions, or tics start suddenly and are accompanied by other behavioral changes and motor abnormalities or handwriting changes. A friend had mentioned PANS, and when she looked into it, Lucy knew immediately this was what Jacob had.

She explained the long path to diagnosis. "Many doctors and therapists think kids are just acting out, and everyone just started to believe Jacob was a bad kid. But as a parent, I knew my son. I knew he wasn't bad. We just had to find him help."

When Jacob was eleven, a pediatric neurologist in Washington, DC, finally confirmed he had PANS. Over the next two years, Jacob had four rounds of IVIG (Intravenous Immunoglobulin) treatments and saw two more PANS specialists, including Dr. Rosario Trifiletti in New Jersey. Dr. Trifiletti did new bloodwork and prescribed antibiotics, antivirals, and diet changes, which usually heal children who have had PANS for a short while.

By the time Jacob saw Dr. Trifiletti, however, he had been living with PANS for ten years. He had already missed the last ten weeks of fifth grade, and he was barely attending school in his first quarter of sixth grade. Lucy and Greg knew Jacob needed more intervention if he was going to be able to resume a normal life. They made the loving yet difficult decision to send him to a therapeutic wilderness program in order to receive intensive therapy with counselors and teachers.

For so long, PANS and Jacob had been Lucy's focus, but now she knew there was another mystery she must solve. "I need to find Ellie," she told me. "I need to know what happened to my twin."

When she heard me speak about homelessness, it amplified a whisper she was already hearing to find out what happened to her sister. Lucy and Ellie were about to turn forty-five. It had been almost twenty years since Ellie, once her best friend, had been in her life. She could not bear the thought that their momentous birthday was coming and she had no idea where Ellie might be. She knew she had to listen to that whisper to find Ellie.

"Do you think you could help?" Lucy asked me.

I didn't know if I could, but I knew someone who might be able to. Liz Clasen-Kelly was well-connected with homeless services not only in Charlotte but throughout the state. She could access the many databases and networks that tried to track people experiencing homelessness. I knew she might be able to find Ellie, but I also knew that searching might come with risks.

"I know someone I can call to help you," I told Lucy. "But you need to be prepared. Ellie could be dead, or she could be in bad shape. Even if she is not, she might not want to talk with you once you find her. Are you sure you are ready for any one of those outcomes?"

Lucy did not hesitate. "Yes, I need to know. I have to find Ellie or at least know I tried."

In an email to Liz, I explained Lucy's story and asked for her help to find Ellie. Liz was more than familiar with family members looking for loved ones who had disappeared into homelessness. Over the years, mothers, fathers, and siblings would call Roof Above homeless services searching for sisters, brothers, sons, and daughters.

It did not take her long to find some evidence that Ellie was alive in Raleigh—just a few hours from Charlotte but still a world away for someone with no resources and no transportation. Through an online search, she was even able to find a tragic mugshot of Ellie—a wide-eyed woman in a torn shirt and disheveled graying hair staring lifelessly at the camera. With circles under her eyes, Ellie appeared exhausted. It was difficult to imagine she was Lucy's twin.

Liz also found that Ellie had been receiving help at a women's center, so that was the most likely place to begin. Armed with this new information from Liz, Lucy finally had a starting place to solve the twenty-year mystery. She also discovered from Ellie's records that a public defender had recently negotiated a plea deal for her sister to enter a transitional facility for women experiencing homelessness rather than go to prison. Lucy made a list of all such facilities in the Raleigh area and began calling. Miraculously, on her second call, she found where Ellie was staying.

Lucy left message after message for her sister, but her calls were never returned. After a few tries, she enlisted Ashley, a dear friend of both twins from high school who lived near Raleigh, to go speak to Ellie in person on Lucy's behalf. Ashley was able to reach Ellie and give her Lucy's phone number.

Lucy still remembers the message she received on November 29, 2017. On that day she was far from North Carolina, visiting Jacob, who was finally beginning to heal from PANS at the wilderness therapy camp. After more than two decades of no contact with her sister, Lucy believed it was no coincidence that she received a voicemail from her twin, Ellie, on the very same day she visited her son, Jacob, for the first time after he had been away from home for six weeks.

"He was healing," Lucy wrote me, her email punctuated with disbelief and excitement at the miracle of both finding Ellie and witnessing her son's recovery. "That day proved to me that Jacob's healing and Ellie's healing were so clearly linked on a larger cosmic level."

After Ellie left her a voicemail, Lucy drove to meet her sister in a tearful reunion that once again bonded the sisters and restored their family tie. Ellie has now become a part of Lucy's family again, and a proud aunt to the niece and nephew she never knew about.

Like Lucy, I believed it all had to be connected. I didn't think it was an accident that she heard me speak about homelessness at the same time her whisper began to *Find Ellie*. Lucy emailed me:

I could feel something shift in my life after we met for coffee. Spending time with you [and] hearing your story about your mom and her bipolar disorder not only helped me reconnect with Ellie but also helped me make some bold decisions in other areas of my life with my son, Jacob.

For me, Lucy was another God Dot in my life who helped deepen my growing belief about these divine connections. When we experience such incredible moments of serendipity and dismiss them as coincidence, we are also dismissing the true miracle attached. I don't believe we are hurtling alone on this planet. We not only have each other but have a God intricately weaving us toward each other. The divine connections are all around us, just waiting to be noticed.

Lucy agreed. "I'm not sure how it will all unfold, but I am staying open to whatever God Dots occur in my life," she wrote.

After almost two decades apart, she is still amazed that she found Ellie and regained a relationship with the person most dear to her. She doesn't quite know what to make of it all, but she believes,

This is what I know for sure. . . . When we listen to our intuition and start living our true-life purpose, when we make bold choices one step at a time, and when we reach out to others to help them, our circumstances shift. Grace opens up new pathways and miracles occur in ALL areas of our life.

At the time, Lucy believed that finding Ellie was, in itself, miracle enough. But the rest of the story, with all of its God Dot connections, was just beginning to unfold.

13

Molly: The One

Rushing to Moore Place, I was running late for a tour of the facility I had promised to give a group of women from Raleigh who had read my book. This was starting to be a fairly regular occurrence as book clubs and Bible study groups read *The Hundred Story Home*. Most of those who reached out for tours did so simply because the story moved them, and they wanted to walk the halls that had touched their heart.

A small percentage who came, maybe 10 percent, were different and had a rarer reason in mind. These were the people hearing whispers. They weren't just moved—they were changed. Reading the book, they had seen something and now could not unsee it. Once they paid attention, their own whispers formed from Denver's questions.

Where are the beds?

You mean to tell me you do all this good in the day and lock 'em out to the bad at night?

Does that make any sense to you?

Are you *going to do something about it?*

These were the people I loved to meet and encourage—those who not only saw the problem differently but felt called to *do something* about it. Within this subset I was starting to see a pattern of people whom I liked to call "the one," individuals like Caroline Bundy, with her idea of the Way Station, Betsy Blue with HopeWay, and Jackie Craig with The Green Chair Project. They knew it was no longer a choice. Their whisper had become so insistent they had to *do something*—whatever that something was.

For "the one," the whisper wasn't a should. It was a *must*. These few could no longer pretend they didn't hear that whisper, no matter how inconvenient, unexpected, and uncomfortable it was to listen.

* * * *

As I hurried into Moore Place, I was confident this group was part of the 90 percent—nice women from a book club who thought it might be fun to see the place they'd read so much about. When I received an email a few weeks before from the leader of this group, Molly Painter, she mentioned she was a friend of someone at Green Chair.

My assumption was that they were driving to Charlotte, having lunch, touring Moore Place, and driving back to Raleigh. I imagined they would talk on the way home about all they saw, and then mostly forget all about it by the next day. When I went to meet Molly and company, I did not think she was "the one." The *one* who would not only hear a whisper but heed it in Raleigh.

I was, of course, completely wrong.

Molly and her three friends were waiting for me in the sunlit lobby. There is a two-story glass wall in the entrance that fills the space with natural light. This architectural feature usually surprises visitors, who expect a building created for formerly homeless men and women to be more of a no-frills, cinder block warehouse. Molly seemed a little shy for a leader as we made introductions. But even though she was quiet, she stood out from the group because she seemed to radiate kindness. With shoulder-length blond hair and light blue eyes that reminded me a little of Frances Hailey's aquamarine eyes, Molly appeared as lovely on the outside as she was on the inside.

As we toured Moore Place, Molly was very comfortable connecting with residents, which was not always the case. On past tours, some people interacted easily with staff but were not sure how to talk with residents. Molly spoke very naturally with everyone, and I noticed she was also furiously writing down notes.

I was hurrying our tour along because I had planned on this meeting taking precisely one hour so that I could get downtown for another appointment. When we had about twenty minutes remaining, I was still sure I could keep to my tight schedule.

We gathered in the Moore Place dining hall for questions and sat in folding chairs along a six-foot table. I still believed this was just a mildly interested group of friends. But then Molly began asking questions, and I could see there was so much more to her story.

"We all help at the women's shelter in Raleigh," she said. "It began with just volunteering to bring coffee for the women. And then Katie here started making cappuccinos and lattes!"

The four women all laughed about their shared experience, which I still did not quite understand.

"So, you run something like a Starbucks at the shelter?" I asked.

"We do, but it is so much more," Molly explained. "We give the women a choice—a small choice, like either vanilla syrup or hazelnut. It is so heartbreaking to see how much that matters. These women have so few choices in their lives right now."

Molly's friends nodded as they began sharing stories of their coffee time and the women they had come to know. They smiled and teared up all at the same time, talking about what they had learned and how they were now seeing things so very differently. Just like the soup kitchen when I had volunteered there years ago, this women's shelter offered a lot of help in the day but not at night. Molly and her friends were understanding what Denver Moore had shown me—that day ministries inherently but unintentionally "lock 'em out to the bad at night."

As she explained, Molly's tears spilled over. "When we arrive in the mornings, some of the women have spent the night behind the building. Their blankets and sleeping bags are soaking wet. We try to help. We have even paid for hotels some nights, but it isn't enough." Her voice caught, and she shook her head, saying softly again, "It just isn't enough!"

As Molly tried to keep from crying, it was obvious that what was happening to the women she helped serve was breaking her heart. She was seeing something in a way that she could no longer unsee it. I was finally seeing something too.

Molly was *the one*. She and her friends were not simply a drive-by book club group who were going to marvel at Moore Place and go home. They were going to do something about it.

Looking at my watch, I panicked when I saw the time. I had to leave, but really, I needed to stay. Molly was exactly the type of person, the *one*, I wanted to talk with, because, like Caroline Bundy, I understood exactly how she was feeling. I wanted to tell Molly that she should pay attention to what she was hearing, even though it might feel unlikely that she should listen. I needed her to believe without a doubt that she should *trust the whisper*. But there was no time; I had to leave for my appointment.

"I am so sorry," I told her, trying to explain my mistake. "I thought you all just wanted to see Moore Place. I didn't understand you were actually trying to *build* one in Raleigh! I do want to help you, but I have to leave for another meeting."

They were gracious as we hugged goodbye, and I promised more follow-up via email. As I drove away, I felt heartsick about how I'd missed this one. Molly was exactly the kind of person I'd hoped my book might find—another one of the "ten" people meant to read it—and miraculously, it had ended up in her hands. But even though she'd been right in front of me, I'd been too overscheduled to help her.

The rest of the day flew by, and that night I didn't have time to send the promised email. When I woke up around 5:30 the next morning, it felt as if my mind had worked all night to connect the God Dots for me as I slept.

Raleigh.

Serving coffee at the shelter.

All the stories of the women they are helping.

Ellie, Lucy's twin sister, is homeless in Raleigh.

What if Molly and her friends have been serving coffee and helping Ellie?

My eyes flew open, and I jumped out of bed. Could it be possible that Molly and her friends knew Ellie? Grabbing my computer, I began typing an email that started with an apology and moved to encouragement for what they were about to undertake. Beginning my email with "Dear Team Raleigh," I wrote, in part:

> I don't know what you are ultimately called to do, but I can tell without a doubt, from meeting and listening to you, that you are on the right path. Whether you sublease a few apartments or someday build a building or start a Housing First nonprofit, it will be lifesaving for someone, and no life is expendable. I know we talked about a lot of numbers and facts and terms about permanent supportive housing and vouchers, which can be overwhelming. But remember, eleven years ago I couldn't have told you any of that. I only knew what you know today—that it can't be right for people, women especially, to have no place to call home.

My apology was running eight paragraphs. I knew I was bordering on overwhelming rather than encouraging. I finally ended my email with my question:

> There is a grace both in this work and in this world. You have already felt how transforming it can be. I am grateful every day it found me

and I listened. Keep listening and following all the God Dots in your lives. You are already connecting them in powerful ways.

There is one dot I am curious if we should have connected yesterday. Let me know if one of the homeless women you have come across in Raleigh is named Ellie. It's possible she goes by another name, so I've put her photo below. If you know her, or come across her, that is a whole other God story.

When I finished typing, I attached the photo Liz Clasen-Kelly had found and sent to Lucy. I knew it was unlikely Molly would actually know Lucy's twin sister, but then again, I had come to believe daily miracles were all around us, just waiting to be noticed.

By the time I took a shower and returned to my computer, the miracle was waiting for me. Each of the four women from Team Raleigh had already responded.

We DO know sweet Ellie and would love to know her story! Katie and Molly are serving coffee this morning at the women's center, and Ellie is probably there.

We see her every week! I am heading there now and will send you a return picture. Running late, as always. So much more to say . . .

I have chills from reading your email. Yes! Ellie is a friend of ours! She has told me that she has a sister in Charlotte. I have always had a special place in my heart for her.

And this was Molly's reply:

My daughter read your email out loud to me in the car as I was driving, and we were both sobbing. This is the most amazing connection! It just blows my mind what God can do! I would love to connect with Lucy and share Ellie stories! It's just too much to put into words! I texted our group that it has definitely been a WOW kind of week, and this is the BIG WOW.

It was beyond miraculous that Molly and her friends knew Ellie and I knew her long-lost twin sister, and that somehow we were all now connected. That was some amazing grace.

I could not wait to tell Lucy the incredible news that I had met Molly and her friends. When I called, she was on a run but picked up my call anyway. She sounded out of breath, and I know I was out of breath as well, speaking fast to connect the God Dots on how I had come to know four women in Raleigh who knew and loved her sister.

Listening to the story, Lucy was as stunned as I had been, and she began to cry. "That has been the worst part—knowing Ellie was homeless and imagining that no one cared about her," she said. "And now to know that there are women there who care about her and love her? Just amazing."

She and I marveled together at the odds of all this lining up, and I promised to connect her with Molly and her friends, now firmly named "Team Raleigh."

Lucy wrote them, in part:

Team Raleigh—I am so, so grateful for all of you. Thank you for loving my sweet sister, Ellie.

Ellie and I email each other a lot, and today I told her that I connected with you. She adores all of you and was excited to hear that we have connected!

Ellie blames herself for her current situation and claims she was lazy and made bad decisions, because that's what my parents have told her over and over again. So, Ellie has taken this on as her "story," but it's not the truth. Ellie is a survivor, and she has done the best she can with the circumstances she found herself in.

I told Ellie today that I would love to come to Raleigh for a visit again this summer, and maybe meet some of you. Hopefully we can work that out.

Over the next few months, Lucy, Ellie, and Team Raleigh did meet. Molly continued following her whisper to build housing in

Raleigh, driven in part by helping women like Ellie. For Lucy, all the connections felt like a miracle.

> Finding Ellie after not having any contact with her for over twenty years was a miracle that unfolded before my eyes. There were many times I thought I would never see her again, but I always held a tiny bit of hope. Finding her was absolute proof to me that all things are truly possible, that everything is connected, and that miracles abound but we just have to look for them.

> When we set an intention that is aligned with our highest good, and we take some type of action steps toward it, [I believe] the universe steps in and helps make it a reality. It's as if the universe literally creates a cascade of miracles to make it so.

14

Liz: Saving Isaac

The remarkable relationship between Team Raleigh, Lucy, and Ellie was a story about which I couldn't stop shaking my head in wonder. How did all those pieces come together?

Then another God Dot connection between Liz Clasen-Kelly and Lucy Fields made it all even more miraculous.

Looking back, Liz and I realized the next piece of the story began months earlier. It was the morning we gave a tour of Moore Place to Miss Jo and her Kingsport delegation. On that same morning, before she hurried to meet us, Liz had a tough time getting her five-year-old son, Isaac, dressed for school. It had been a chilly November day, and Liz remembers trying to pull a long-sleeve shirt over his head, but Isaac was not having it.

Her normally sweet and compliant son was defiant, raging even, as he fought his mother. "I can't wear long sleeves and pants anymore!"

She was frustrated and eventually lost the battle to her son, allowing him to go to school with short sleeves and a jacket.

Eventually, with all the excitement of the day touring with Miss Jo, Liz forgot about her morning struggle.

Later that same day, she and her husband, Fred, took Isaac to see a Charlotte Hornets basketball game. It was one of their favorite family outings, but that night the team lost—and oddly, Isaac was inconsolable. Fred was carrying him to the car when he began fighting his dad, and they had a horrible time getting him into the car seat. "He wailed from the arena to the parking lot and all the way home," Liz recalled.

It was even difficult to get Isaac to sleep, but Liz was not yet worried. She just thought he was having a "terrible twos" kind of day even though he was five years old. However, her worries escalated over the next few days.

Like *Groundhog Day*, that same tantrum now played out every single morning, and Isaac had become prone to fits of rage. While he could hold it together at school, he was a terror at home.

"It was as if overnight, Isaac disappeared and he became possessed," Liz said. "I didn't know what was wrong with him, but I knew something was terribly wrong."

Isaac would not sleep, and everything upset him. He would scream at his parents and even become physically violent. He also had unusual behaviors, becoming obsessed about which clothes he would wear and how they fit his body. They had a family dog, and he abruptly could not stand to have a single dog hair on his clothing. "We had to travel with those sticky hair removers everywhere we went," Liz said.

Liz and Fred tried everything they knew, from time-out punishment to confining Isaac to his room. Liz remembers painstakingly creating a good behavior sticker chart to help incentivize him, but he immediately tore it up. His behavior became so terrifying that on one particularly destructive evening, they called a Crisis Intervention team Liz knew about from her work. They suggested taking Isaac to a mental health hospital, but Fred couldn't do it. He had just written a series for the newspaper on the abuses occurring within child and adolescent mental health centers. He told Liz, "Whatever we do, we are not taking him there."

Within a few days, a child therapist and a behavioral doctor saw Isaac, but still they had no clear diagnosis. What was happening to their son? Exhausted and defeated, Fred and Liz could not imagine where they could find answers. Over five weeks had passed since the night of the Hornets game, and no one in their home was sleeping. They found the only way to help Isaac sleep was to drive him around the neighborhood like a baby with colic. Fred would make circles in the car with Isaac in the back seat, hoping that when he nodded off the madness would finally stop.

To make matters worse, Liz's job could not have been more stressful. At the same time Isaac was throwing unexplained tantrums, she was being considered for a huge career opportunity: CEO of a newly merged nonprofit that would be the largest homeless service organization in the state of North Carolina.

"I need to pull my name from consideration," she told Fred one night. She was functioning on fumes, dealing with work all day and Isaac all night. "I can't do this anymore."

Fred shook his head. "Liz, you were born for this job. If I have to quit my job to take care of Isaac, then that's what we will do. But you are going to interview for that job."

Although Liz and I had been working together often during that hellish month, I did not know what was happening with Isaac. One morning, however, we were supposed to meet, but she called me an hour before to cancel. "I am so sorry. I am not going to be able to meet this morning."

Liz's normally upbeat voice sounded strained and flat.

"Is everything okay?" I asked.

"No, not really," she admitted.

Through tears, Liz gave me a quick overview of the last five weeks. "Isaac throws tantrums and doesn't sleep. We are exhausted and don't know what to do. Fred and I are headed to another doctor appointment," she said. "I think they are finally going to name whatever this is, and I have done some research. It is going to be a tough diagnosis for us and Isaac."

She left out much of the story in an effort to protect her son. What mother wants to believe her child is uncontrollable or has early onset mental health issues? However, though she only told me a few pieces of the story, I had heard a similar one before.

Liz and her son, Isaac.

Lucy and her son, Jacob.

Could it be possible that Isaac and Jacob shared the same diagnosis? That connection felt like a long shot. There were so many potential diagnoses. Why would Isaac have the same rare autoimmune disease as Jacob?

But I had an immediate sense it might be true. In the moment, I could not tell Liz any of that, so I just said, "When you get the diagnosis, call me back. I think I know another mom who can help you, and you already know her."

It was a cryptic message, but I wanted to be certain it was true before I told her the full story. Two hours later, Liz called back, and I knew what she was going to say even before she spoke.

"Have you ever heard of PANS?"

That familiar full-body tingle flooded through me.

Why, yes, I had.

"Liz, you are not going to believe this, but remember Lucy? You helped find her twin sister, Ellie?"

She remembered.

"When we first met, she told me this terrible story about her son, Jacob, and it was exactly how you described Isaac. Wild tantrums that started almost overnight, out of nowhere. It has taken them almost ten years to figure out why, but it's the exact same diagnosis," I told her. "Jacob and Isaac both have PANS."

Liz couldn't believe it. I could hardly believe it myself. What kind of crazy connection was that, not to mention the biblical symmetry in the names of their children—Jacob and Isaac?

"You need to call Lucy," I said. "After ten years of dealing with this, she's practically a world-class expert. I know she found the most amazing doctor somewhere, and it won't take you ten years to find help for Isaac."

She started crying, and I was tearing up as well. Liz had met Lucy at a time in her life when Lucy had rarely spoken about Ellie but needed help. Now, a year later, Liz had let few people know what was happening in her home, but she needed help for Isaac.

"It struck me as truly sacred that we got to meet each other in our most vulnerable moments and be there for each other," Liz told me later about her connection with Lucy.

That very afternoon, Liz and Lucy had a long talk about PANS. Lucy encouraged Liz to let go of the shame of feeling that she was not a good parent and not worry what others thought when Isaac was not behaving properly.

"Your next step is to survive until Isaac can get well," Lucy told her.

She also told Liz all about Dr. Rosario Trifiletti. He had treated more than five thousand children from all over the world and had become a leading expert in this newly recognized yet still controversial diagnosis. Through his research, Dr. Trifiletti had discovered children with PANS were victims of an insidious autoimmune disease that attacked the part of the brain responsible for OCD and psychotic symptoms. Normally there was a long wait time to get an appointment with him, but when Liz called there had just been a cancellation.

"Can you be here Tuesday?" the receptionist asked Liz.

Liz, Fred, and Isaac made the long car ride to New Jersey, but not without incident. Isaac had to be restrained as he fought Liz and even tried to escape from the car. "That car ride was just hell," she remembered.

When they saw Dr. Trifiletti, however, things began to change. Dr. Trifiletti suspected Isaac had both PANS and walking pneumonia, which can also be an indicator of a PANS infection.

111

"I knew we were all tired and feeling terrible," Liz said. "But I just thought Isaac had a cold and was delirious from not sleeping."

Ten days later, when all the blood work came back, Isaac was officially diagnosed with PANS, and the pneumonia was confirmed as well. Dr. Trifiletti started a series of antibiotics and dietary changes that slowly began to restore Isaac to his former self. The tantrums subsided, and Fred no longer had to drive him around the neighborhood at night.

"I have my son back," Liz said months later, in tears. "Meeting Lucy meant we got a shortcut through all this."

Lucy told her, "You need to be doing other things, so I believe God gave you that shortcut."

It would take almost a year and a half for Isaac to fully recover, but that was far less than the ten years Jacob suffered, and less than many other families dealing with a PANS diagnosis.

"I wish Isaac never had to go through all that, because he did lose a huge part of his childhood," Liz said. "Our path was really hard and really painful, but we were never alone."

She also came to believe that somehow that painful path was one she was meant to walk, yet she wrestled with why some people received healing and others didn't. "If I get to ask God questions at the end, that will be my first question. I will ask God about healing," she said, and also wondered why their path was easier. "Theologically, I don't understand it, but I know Lucy was a huge part of reminding me God was in it."

Liz had been the God Dot Lucy needed to find Ellie.

Lucy had been the God Dot Liz needed to save Isaac.

Neither Liz nor Lucy believed they did anything particularly difficult or heroic for the other. They simply offered their expertise and shared what they knew. But each became a very holy part of the other's story.

"We are all vessels," Liz said. "We all get invited into this larger story if we choose to listen."

15

Bill: The LifeVest

Maybe the reason I was so taken by Liz and Lucy and their God Dot connection was because my husband, Charlie, and I were also dealing with a rare disease.

The year after Moore Place opened, Charlie and I had been visiting our daughter, Emma, at her school near Boston. It was a cold, snowy Friday, so Charlie went to the hotel gym instead of taking his usual jog outside. Had it not been snowing, I am sure Charlie would have been running outside, and what happened next would've had a very different ending.

My husband was an adrenaline junkie who loved every heart-pumping sport: running, tennis, and even heli-skiing. At the time, he was fifty-three years old but could pass for a man in his thirties. Incredibly toned and fit, Charlie would never sit still if he had a chance to exercise in some way. I tended to find every excuse *not* to exercise, so on that snowy afternoon, I was in our hotel room reading emails.

He had only left for the gym twenty minutes earlier, so I was surprised to see him back in our room so quickly. But as the door closed behind him, he shuffled past me, clutching his upper arms in obvious distress.

I could barely hear him when he said, "I am so tired. I think I will take a nap."

As he spoke, Charlie fell heavily onto the stiff hotel mattress, his right hand resting on his chest and his impossibly long legs hanging over the side of the bed, not quite touching the floor. While I was surprised that he would ever leave a gym before finishing his workout, I was not immediately concerned. He had recently visited a cardiologist for some persistent chest and arm pain, but he was told his symptoms were simply the result of stress.

I did stand up to take a better look, and when I did I could see his eyes were closed as he rested, but what shocked me were his hands. They were ghostly white, as if no blood was circulating beneath the skin.

I tried to keep the panic out of my voice. "Charlie, you need to get up. I think we need to see a doctor."

From that moment, our lives were never the same again.

I managed to get Charlie into our rental car and found an urgent care center nearby. From there, we were suddenly in a speeding ambulance, as Charlie's unmoving body was rushed into surgery.

Completely alone in the hospital waiting room, I collapsed in shock. How did we go from hotel to urgent care to ambulance to ER in under sixty minutes? I didn't even know the name of the hospital we were in, only that we were somewhere near Boston, in Lowell, Massachusetts.

I have no idea how long I waited before a nurse came to tell me, "Your husband has had a heart attack."

"What?" I shook my head. How could Charlie, the healthiest person I knew, have a heart attack? "When did he have a heart attack?" I asked.

She looked at me funny. "Don't you know that's why you are here?"

I couldn't answer. The last few hours were only a blur.

The nurse reached for my hands. "Your husband's main artery, it's called the LAD, the left anterior descending artery, was blocked, and it caused a heart attack," she said.

I shook my head as she said those words, *heart attack*, again, and I tried to understand how that was possible.

"We are not yet sure why it happened, but you are very lucky that Dr. Ali was on call," the nurse continued. "He was able to put two stents in your husband's heart. We think he is going to make it."

We think he is going to make it.

Over the next few days, in a Massachusetts cardiac ICU, we would come to understand just how extraordinarily lucky we had been that day. When we arrived at the hospital, Charlie's main cardiac artery had completely collapsed, which had caused his heart attack. It turned out, however, that the true cause was not heart disease but a rare disease called SCAD—Spontaneous Coronary Artery Dissection. The doctor who had saved Charlie's life, Dr. Omar Ali, had a lot to explain to us.

"Typically, a blockage is caused by plaque, but your arteries, Charlie, they are pristine, truly pristine," Dr. Ali marveled. "Your blockage was caused by something very rare—it spontaneously dissected."

While it was difficult to understand how someone as healthy as Charlie could have had a heart attack, Dr. Ali wanted us to understand the real miracle was that he was alive.

"Some call that particular artery the widow maker, because when it is blocked without immediate intervention, survival rates can be very low," Dr. Ali said. "A dissection of the LAD is unusual, especially in males, and it typically would be discovered only after an autopsy."

Autopsy. That word stopped me cold. Dr. Ali was trying to say that Charlie should be dead but somehow, against all odds, was alive.

"What happened today is what we call a 'black swan event.' It hardly ever happens," Dr. Ali told us. "I have only seen one in my career. Charlie, you are very lucky to be here."

Was this some type of God Dot connection as well, that Charlie had survived the unsurvivable? I could not say, and I was too worried about too many other things to really consider it at the time.

We had so much yet to learn about SCAD, but Dr. Ali immediately let us know this was not a "one and done" event. With SCAD, patients were at risk of the same thing happening again at any time.

Because Charlie was still groggy from the procedure, I was the only one asking questions and fully comprehending what Dr. Ali was telling us.

"So, you are saying this could happen again?" I asked, still shaken from the ambulance ride and not wanting to ever relive this day.

"Yes," the doctor said. "I am afraid it can."

"Is there a test he could get that would warn us?" I asked.

Dr. Ali shook his head. "Unfortunately, we can only see a dissection after they occur."

"Is there a medicine or a treatment to prevent them?"

Dr. Ali shook his head again. "There are so few people who have SCAD that there is very little research right now, and not much is understood about how to treat it."

It was just beginning to sink in that we had a long road ahead of us, not just learning to live with this rare disease but also worrying about another heart attack. Which led to our first big problem— how were we going to get home?

We were over eight hundred miles from Charlotte. The thought of driving more than fourteen hours was terrifying. What if Charlie had another heart attack while we were on the road? Dr. Ali had told us there was no way to predict why arteries dissected with SCAD, but when they did, Charlie would need to get to a hospital in under an hour. Our ambulance ride had delivered Charlie just in time. Who could say, if it happened again, we would be as lucky?

While flying was an option, what if the plane was in the air when Charlie had another heart attack? We could not expect it to land in time to get Charlie to a hospital.

Dr. Ali was sympathetic to our dilemma and offered a solution. "There is something called a LifeVest that a patient can wear, and it monitors cardiac rhythms. If an arrhythmia begins, the LifeVest delivers a shock treatment to help restore the heart to a normal rhythm until you can get to a hospital."

Dr. Ali wasn't sure how long it might take to get a LifeVest delivered to us, but he offered to help us find out. Charlie had been asleep while we talked about all this, but when he woke up, I explained that somehow we were going to find one of these Life-Vests for our trip home.

"I played golf with that guy," Charlie said.

Since he was still on several medications from his procedure, I wasn't sure if Charlie was making sense or not. "You played golf with what guy?" I asked.

"The LifeVest guy. The guy who is the CEO of that company," Charlie said.

That seemed way too small-world and serendipitous to believe. Charlie just happened to play golf with someone who would not only know how to get a LifeVest but was CEO of the company that made them?

Even through his anesthetic haze, Charlie was adamant this was true. He insisted he had recently played in a foursome where one of the guys worked for a medical device corporation. While it had not seemed important at the time, Charlie remembered the guy talking about a product his company made called a LifeVest.

It felt improbable, but our best shot was to get the lifesaving device quickly so we could get Charlie home. I wasn't sure how I would find "some guy" that Charlie played golf with, but he knew.

"Bill Whelan will know how to reach him," Charlie said.

Bill was one of Charlie's business partners who worked in Boston. Apparently, he knew the LifeVest guy, and he had been the one who invited Charlie to play with them on a recent golf outing.

"I'll reach out to Bill," Charlie said, but then he closed his eyes to take another nap.

"I'll call him," I said, taking Charlie's cell phone from his too-tired hand.

Stepping out of the hospital ICU room, I began searching for Bill's phone number. I saw a man in the hall, looking as if he were trying to find a patient's room. As he turned around to face me, I stared at him in shock.

"Bill?" I said.

Bill Whelan was standing in the hallway in front of me.

"Kathy!" he said. "I've been trying to find Charlie all morning."

As I tried to process how it could be possible that the man I needed to find was somehow standing right in front of me, Bill was already telling me his side of the story.

"None of us could believe it when we heard Charlie had a heart attack. I mean, he's just too healthy," Bill said.

Bill wasn't planning on visiting Charlie in the hospital that morning because he had a full day of meetings at his office in Boston. But when Bill was lying in bed that morning, about to get up and go into Boston, he had a strange thought: *My friend Charlie is lying in a hospital bed this morning. I wonder, does he need anything?*

Bill says it wasn't a vision or a voice, just the strong sense he needed to go see Charlie. "I just couldn't stop thinking about it. I kept having this same thought. 'My partner is in a hospital, and I need to go see him.'"

The problem was, Bill did not know which hospital Charlie was in. Even if he'd called me, I'm not sure I could have told him the name either, since we had come in through the back doors of an emergency room by ambulance. Bill shook his head, remembering how he had gotten in his car and driven to his best guess. That first hospital he went to had no record of Charlie, and they suggested another one. He resolved to keep trying each of the many area hospitals until he found us.

"This was my second try!" Bill laughed.

I hugged him, still not believing he had shown up at exactly the right moment. "I can't believe you are here. Literally, we were just talking about you," I told him, and explained the rest of the story.

When he came into Charlie's hospital room, Charlie was surprised and tried to downplay what had happened. "I am going to be fine!" he said.

But seeing Charlie surrounded by machines and tubes, Bill thought, *You don't look fine, buddy!*

Bill only had to make one call to connect the God Dots, and Charlie was fitted that afternoon with a LifeVest. The very next day, we flew home, feeling surrounded by grace and so grateful to be alive.

I've thought back on that time a lot. We didn't know that first episode in Boston was just the beginning of living in radical uncertainty due to a long string of medical complications over the next ten years. From that moment, we began to recalibrate our lives to living with a rare disease that meant another crucial artery might dissect at any moment, and Charlie might not be so lucky the second time.

There was a lot of medical science that helped Charlie live that day. Dr. Ali had to be superbly trained to repair a fragile, shredded artery and insert two lifesaving stents. But there was also a lot of grace involved as well.

What told me to take Charlie to urgent care and not simply let him take a nap? I now understand that without that whisper, Charlie never would have woken up.

How did a whisper guide Bill to find Charlie among all of the Boston area hospitals?

But even before that, how had the God Dots aligned for Charlie to play golf with the CEO of the very medical device company that made the one product he would need?

. . . .

Years later, I asked Bill for his take on that day and how he felt faith played a part. Raised in a large Catholic family, he still goes to services most Sundays.

"It's my time of reflection," Bill said. "I ask myself if I am living the way God wants me to. And it is also my time of giving thanks for my kids and my grandkids. It's important to me." He doesn't claim to hear God's voice but rather believes, "I have the feeling he is listening."

Ten years ago, when he could have gone into the office instead of searching for Charlie to see if his friend needed anything, Bill believes God was there as well. "I think God was right there with me, nudging me and guiding me."

Often, we try to separate things into being either scientific or spiritual. Francis S. Collins is a physician and geneticist who led the Human Genome Project and was the director of the National Institutes of Health for over thirteen years. In his *New York Times* bestseller, *The Language of God: A Scientist Presents Evidence for Belief*, Collins writes that science and faith can and should coexist.

> In this modern era of cosmology, evolution, and the human ge-
> nome, is there still the possibility of a richly satisfying harmony
> between the scientific and spiritual worldviews? I answer this with
> a resounding yes! In my view, there is no conflict between being a
> rigorous scientist and a person who believes in a God who takes a
> personal interest in each one of us. Science's domain is to explore
> nature. God's domain is the spiritual world, a realm not possible
> to explore without the tools and language of science. It must be
> examined with the heart, the mind, and the soul—and the mind
> must find a way to embrace both realms.[1]

Collins gets to the heart of what so many of us struggle with: How do we embrace both realms? In Charlie's case, I have to believe it was both the skill of a surgeon as well as a few holy whispers that came together for a miracle survival story. This has made me understand that it is not a question of believing in science or faith but, as Collins insists, embracing both realms.

I also asked Bill if he remembered ever receiving any other messages where he felt God was nudging him. He thought for a moment and then said, "I think we can see signs in nature that are very comforting."

Bill, who was raised in a family of six children, said he saw just such a sign after his father died. "There were six red cardinals at our bird feeder—I had never seen that before! I just know it was my dad saying everything was going to be all right."

16

Chris: God's Better Plan

While Charlie's incredible survival felt like a true miracle in our lives, we kept the story fairly private. Only a few friends and family knew the details of his SCAD diagnosis. It was easier just to be grateful that Charlie survived a heart attack and not dwell on the dangers of dissecting arteries. He just wanted to believe it wouldn't happen again, so he went back to the office as if that were true. I tried to put it out of my mind as best I could by distracting myself with work. In public, I was talking about homelessness and mental health. In private, I remained awake at night thinking about heart attacks, medical emergencies, and becoming a widow.

When the pandemic shuttered the world, we added another layer of worry. There was no doctor who could predict how COVID might affect Charlie's fragile arteries and heart. In that first year of the pandemic, we isolated from everyone, trying to keep him safe. With little else to focus on, I began journaling about our life with SCAD. While I never planned to publish any of it, wrestling with worry on the page helped me cope with all the medical mystery in our lives.

As the world socially distanced, I stopped meeting in person with people who wanted to talk about *The Hundred Story Home* or their whispers. But every once in a while, I had a video call to encourage someone, which is how I met Chris Locklear.

When Chris logged on, he was on the back porch of his home in Belmont, North Carolina, and I was in my den in Charlotte. Chris appeared to be a big guy with muscled shoulders, close-cropped hair, and a strong jawline. While he looked pretty tough, Chris let me know in the first five minutes that he might cry.

"I am probably going to get emotional telling you all this," he said. "It is nothing short of a miracle."

I was still unclear what exactly he wanted to talk about, but I had learned to be patient with people explaining their whispers. There was usually a good story behind them.

Chris started at the beginning, telling me he'd grown up in what he described as a middle-class family that was part of the Lumbee Indian tribe. As a boy, Chris dreamed about becoming an engineer and joined his school NASA science club. His nickname was CJ, and he was a three-sport athlete playing basketball, football, and baseball. His parents took him to church often. "We had morals at an early age," he told me.

Chris recounted that his father was ex-military, which made him hard on his children, though his son said it was out of love. The first crack in Chris's strong foundation began in fourth grade, after his parents divorced. Not knowing how to cope, Chris struggled quietly, but it wasn't until high school that his life began to derail. He vividly remembered the downward spiral through drugs and alcohol that took root in tenth grade. Drugs helped numb his pain, and soon nothing mattered.

His first intervention was at the age of nineteen, when he was sent to rehab in Wilmington, North Carolina. This began a cycle of detoxing, receiving treatment, leaving rehab for the complicated real world, and then relapsing, which pushed him further and further down a hole from which he felt he could not escape. Desperate to break the cycle of addiction, he thought moving to Charlotte might give him a fresh chance for a different life. And that is when he dropped his nickname, CJ, and began introducing himself as Chris.

He smiled as he told me, "I wanted the white picket fence life."

In 2002, he boarded a Greyhound bus that turned out to be a one-way ticket to more disappointment. "I ended up homeless in Charlotte," Chris said, and the tears he promised might appear began to well up.

Between 2002 and 2004, Chris spent a lot of time lost and looking for help. He talked about the bridges he slept under, the dumpsters he foraged in, and the railroad tracks leading to no way out. He had a bed in the men's shelter, but then he failed a Breathalyzer test, which forced him out onto the streets again.

"I just felt hopeless," he said.

It was a counselor at the men's shelter named Billy Godwin who first tried to help him find hope. In the small world of fate and God Dots, Billy's son was one of Chris's best friends growing up in Pembroke, North Carolina. When he was a boy, Chris had no idea his friend's dad was a counselor in Charlotte or that they would one day meet at the shelter. Billy, like Chris's dad, was ex-military, and he spoke the hard truth to Chris. "I see potential in you, but you have to want it for yourself."

That connection and encouragement began a winning streak in Chris's life. He got a job at Walmart. An apartment. A new start at the community college where he enrolled in engineering classes. He felt his life was on track again—then a romantic relationship began another series of bad decisions. Chris lost his sobriety, dropped out of school, and became estranged from his family.

"They were exhausted," he said. "They turned me over to God and decided whatever happened to me, they were going to have to live with it."

Almost nine more years passed as he cycled in and out of treatment and homelessness. His lowest point came on a cold February night. He was walking in a snowstorm with no jacket, and he felt he wanted to die. Chris didn't want to live like this anymore. He knew he was either going to die on the streets or end up in prison. He didn't want either one of those options to be the sum of his life, so he believed it would be best if he died that night.

"I asked God once again, please, just don't allow me to wake up," Chris told me.

Even though he tried to end his life with pills and alcohol that night, he did wake up. He found himself in a hospital. His life had once again been saved, this time by emergency workers who found him nearly frozen to death from hypothermia.

When he regained consciousness, Chris remembers being in a rage when he realized he wasn't dead. "Looking back, it's funny how when I begged God to take me out of this world, he didn't. He had a different plan."

Chris left the hospital for another attempt at detox, but this time was different because he was different. The experience had shifted something in him. He began taking the process seriously while working through the traditional twelve steps of Alcoholics Anonymous. His sponsor told him, "Accept your role in this. Your parents divorced when you were in fourth grade, but you are now twenty-nine. Let's stop playing the blame game."

He reconnected with his family, and his dad admitted, "I have prayed for you to come home so many times—just not in a body bag."

Chris realized, "I had spent ten years destroying other people's lives and my own. Now it was time to give back."

He began focusing on living well and repairing the relationships in his life. He earned three levels of nursing certification: CNA, LPN, and RN. Along the way, he made his school's president's list with a plus-4.0 GPA and earned scholarships to pay for all of his education. As president of his LPN nursing class, Chris delivered a speech at his graduation ceremony. Michelle, an incoming nursing student, was in the audience that day and fell in love as she watched him on stage. Eventually, Chris and Michelle married. As we spoke by video chat, he proudly told me he was both a father and a new grandfather, and his name had become "Papa CJ."

Chris was also able to help support his mom, Marilyn Deese, who was battling cancer. An earlier breast cancer diagnosis had returned as bone cancer, spreading to her spine. He went with her for her chemo treatments and watched with pride as she spread hope. "Before we would leave the center, she would connect with the other patients, giving each a Scripture or a message of hope."

When I asked him about all his successes and reconnecting with his family after years of struggle, Chris said, "I didn't want to let anyone down again, especially, and maybe finally, myself."

In April 2019, after years of hopelessness, he finally landed his "dream job" that allowed him to give back to others. "I have been looking for this my whole life," he said. "I can restore hope. I am the assistant director of nursing at HopeWay."

As Chris told me that, it was my turn to tear up.

This is why he wanted to meet with me. He wanted to tell me how the two paths of his life had intersected in such a miraculous way. Chris had been told about my connection to both Roof Above and HopeWay and how those two paths had intersected in my life. He wanted to not only share his story with me but also find out how he might begin volunteering for Roof Above. Chris now wanted to help others know there was hope out of homelessness.

After we spoke, I introduced him to some Roof Above staff, but he would have to wait another year through the pandemic to begin volunteering. By that time, Chris was hearing another whisper, not just to volunteer but to seek employment at Roof Above. He applied for a nursing position and was even offered the job—but then his fear voice spoke up. The job was exactly what he had always wanted, yet it also meant taking a substantial pay cut.

"My wife told me we were blessed and to just take the job, and we would figure out how to pay our bills," he said. "But I prayed about it all weekend and turned it down on Monday. Still, I thought all that day about how my higher power had always been guiding me to give back freely what had been given to me. And so I called them back on Tuesday and asked if the job was still available—they said it was, but I had to say yes right then, on the phone!"

Chris now works full-time as a nursing manager for Roof Above, sharing supervision of over 360 formerly homeless tenants living in apartments throughout Charlotte. He also still works a few part-time shifts at HopeWay. To gain trust and build relationships with his Roof Above tenants, he often shares his story. "I tell them I have slept in a shelter and I have slept under a bridge. They never can believe it."

Chris's story and his deep commitment to the work was one of the feature stories at the 2022 True Blessings luncheon—fifteen years after Denver Moore first spoke. Chris goes the extra mile for his clients, especially some who are cancer patients. His mom lost her own battle with cancer at age sixty-seven, and Chris thinks of her whenever he enters the cancer treatment center with his clients. Often he waits for four to five hours as they receive their chemotherapy, and he has lots of time to reflect. "I still have these days when a tear falls from my eye," he said. "I think a lot about grace and mercy. I feel like God always said if you do the possible, I will do the impossible."

He remembered all the times he asked God to take his life and also the Garth Brooks song "Unanswered Prayers."

"I am so glad God didn't answer my prayers to die," Chris said. "He had a better plan all along."

17

Julia: Prayers in the Park

Chris's story was one of the many that kept me writing and reflecting as the pandemic wore on. Eventually, I wrote down not only the entire story of what happened with Charlie's rare disease but, more importantly, how it shaped us.

When I first started writing, I thought that work was only for my own understanding, and maybe one day it might help our daughters understand their dad's illness. In the process, I read dozens of books on grief, widowhood, death, and life. I wove much of what I learned from over thirty-five authors, poets, and theologians into what became a full-length manuscript titled *The Last Ordinary Hour: Living Life Now That Nothing Will Ever Be the Same.*

Once again, I felt like there had to be at least ten people who needed to read our story about life with a rare disease in order to help them with their own medical uncertainty. I had no idea one of those first ten readers I would hear from would be Julia Robinson.

Julia and I had met a few years before, when I spoke about homelessness at her Greensboro, North Carolina, church. Julia and her husband, Jay, were part of a group called Prayers in the Park, and that name exactly described their mission—they offered prayers in a local park for people experiencing homelessness.

Before my presentation to the whole congregation, I met with Julia and her small prayer group to learn about their ministry. She was memorable to me because of her honesty and reflection about how this ministry had grown. She admitted the original goal was to bring spiritual comfort, but the Prayers in the Park team quickly realized more was needed.

"The people said prayers were nice, but could we bring them some water?" Julia remembered. So the team began including water bottles on their Sunday visits. As they got to know the men and women huddled inside their tents and sleeping bags, it was obvious there were more urgent needs than water.

"They weren't just thirsty, they were really hungry," Julia said.

The Prayers in the Park ministry began extending some Southern hospitality through meals as well. One church member later wrote me about Julia: "She and her husband, Jay, have been tirelessly providing light, love, and bagged lunches."

As I talked with Julia and the other volunteers, I grew increasingly uncomfortable, knowing that my prepared talk might be a little deflating to this ministry. My presentation included how I'd been just like them a decade before, serving soup and a smile to those experiencing homelessness. But just like soup wasn't enough, prayers, water, and bagged lunches were not enough either. What people who were experiencing homelessness actually needed were homes. But even in my discomfort, I was starting to feel as if Julia was *the one*. Like Molly Painter or Lesley Faulkner in her yellow pants, she was going to begin hearing a whisper that day.

Sure enough, after my presentation to the congregation where I talked about Denver asking me about the beds, she walked up to me with tears in her huge hazel eyes.

"Prayers aren't enough, are they?" Julia asked.

I smiled and shook my head.

129

"I am going to have to do more, aren't I?" It wasn't really a question; she already knew the answer and was already listening to the whisper beginning to roar inside her.

I had my own whisper about Julia, so after I returned to Charlotte, I wrote her an encouraging email:

I just have a feeling we should stay in touch, so here is my email. Reach out anytime—you are not crazy, and I think you are already feeling called.

Julia replied early the next morning, writing in part:

I kept my husband up way too late on Monday just talking and dreaming about what I can do to make a difference.

Over the next few months, we exchanged emails as she and Jay moved deeper into the mission of housing, and I learned more about them. They had met in college at Appalachian State when she was eighteen and he was nineteen. After marrying, they had one daughter, Sloan, and a son, Coleman, and raised their children with a big circle of friends and family.

"It was not always rainbows and butterflies," Julia wrote me later, "but when it was good it was great." She felt it was a true gift to be married to her soulmate, and she wanted their children to see the love they had for each other and for God in their lives.

Maybe that is why Julia was ready to listen to her whisper and set an example for her young adult children about giving back in the community. Within the year, she came to Charlotte to tour Moore Place, and afterward she wrote, "I hear the whispers and thank you for turning up the volume in my story."

Jay and some business partners had a portfolio of rental homes, and Julia and Jay began exploring how those properties might help house more people in Greensboro. Over the next year, she and I saw each other two more times, but we did not keep in close touch.

A couple years after we first met, I was surprised to receive an Instagram message from her:

> Reading your book, *The Last Ordinary Hour*. I am
> living this now—Jay was in a horrible ski accident.

As we exchanged texts, I learned Julia and Jay had been on a ski vacation visiting Sloan, who had moved to Colorado. While they were skiing, a snowboarder hit Jay from behind, slamming him into a tree. Luckily, he had been wearing a helmet that saved him from a brain injury, but his internal organs were severely damaged. After forty-eight days, Jay was still in an ICU ward in a Colorado hospital. I remember staring at the screen in shock about the horrible news of the accident, struck by the memory of being exactly where Julia was now, in a hospital watching her husband fight for his life.

She told me more about Jay's accident, and we shared the anxiety of worrying about an unexpectedly injured husband, especially one who had been incredibly healthy. Julia told me that he'd already lost a kidney, but she was confident he would recover.

By the time she reached out to me, Jay had already been in the ICU at St. Anthony's in Lakewood, Colorado, for almost two months. She was both optimistic and exhausted. It helped to have her daughter right there, but most of their family and friends were a thousand miles away in North Carolina. Two dear friends began flying to Colorado every other week to support her, but the weeks were stretching into exhausting months. Although I had experienced the stress of being in an out-of-town ICU with Charlie's first heart attack, we had been able to go home after a week. I couldn't imagine packing for a vacation and two months later still being in an ICU.

Julia hoped June would be the month they could finally get Jay back home to Greensboro. Then on June 15, 2021, at 9:46 p.m., I looked at my phone to see this message:

> He's not going to make it—his liver is shutting
> down.

Staring at my phone in utter shock, I couldn't understand how a healthy guy like Jay could go on a ski vacation and never come home. Julia had been so hopeful the last time we talked. I had no idea what I would say to her, but I dialed her number, if only to leave a message. She picked up my call right away.

I wanted not to cry. I wanted to be that strong friend who somehow gave her strength from thousands of miles away. But when I heard her voice, I immediately started crying, and she began crying as well. Even through her tears, she was unbelievably poised and reflective, given what was about to happen.

"You know, Sloan and I were talking at dinner about what this could all mean," she said. "I mean, what could God's plan possibly be in all this?"

"I know," I told her. "I have been thinking the same. I don't believe there is a reason for everything, but I have been trying to find some meaning somewhere."

"We were thinking that maybe Jay should have died that day on the ski slope, but he didn't," Julia said. "If that had happened, I would have been so bitter and angry, and I don't know that I would have ever gotten over that anger. But we've had all this time with him."

I nodded silently, tears rolling down my cheeks.

"Seventy-seven days," she told me. "He lived in this hospital seventy-seven days."

"Maybe Jay has just been hanging on to be sure you are okay and to have time for you to say all the things you needed to say," I said.

Julia had already considered that. "Two days ago, he kind of woke up," she said. "He hugged us and kissed us and told us he loved us, and we got to tell him how much we loved him."

We held that image between us. If Jay had died instantly on the slope, his family would not have had that moment. Then Julia said, "I told him it was okay to go."

That image of saying goodbye to a soulmate of a husband was exactly what I had been worrying about for more than ten years.

I had played that image over and over in my head, knowing there might come a day when Charlie's SCAD caused another heart attack or a stroke with worse outcomes. I knew someday I might also have to say to my husband in an ICU, "It's okay to go."

Julia and her family were told Jay could be kept alive, but it would be only by machines. It would be a life lived in a hospital. He would never leave that Colorado medical center, never be able to go home to Greensboro.

The next morning, Julia, Sloan, Coleman, her future son-in-law, Conner, and all the nurses and doctors who had cared for Jay at St. Anthony's did something that had never been done before at that hospital. They wheeled Jay's bed up to the helicopter pad on the hospital roof. Together, their whole family and the entire medical team, who had become like family, watched the sunrise. Together, they took in the majesty of another day, and later that morning, they said a final goodbye.

That moment on the roof was captured in photos taken by a nurse who had cared for Jay all those months. Only two years before, Julia had taken a similar photo of Jay viewing a sunset on a North Carolina beach. His lean muscled body was silhouetted by the bright sun, his arms stretched above his head, holding a towel as if running a victory lap. Unlike that ocean-sunset photo with Jay's arms stretched triumphantly above his head, the scene from the hospital roof shows Jay's arms folded at his sides. But he was surrounded by a love as present and visible as the beauty of the sunrise.

I don't think there is a way to look at that photo of Julia's family at that moment without crying. It reveals an overwhelming love of family and an undeniable love of life. Those things are the essence of all this life means. To be in this world with people we love for a finite amount of time. To have and to hold all that is so precious, and yet know we must say goodbye. We will lose those we love, and sometimes the most loving thing we can do is to help those we love leave.

. . . .

Four years prior, I thought my God Dot connection with Julia was about a whisper to do something to create housing for the homeless in Greensboro. And then I believed our God Dot connection was so that I could help her find hope in the hospital.

But now it seems to me that God had a much more intricate plan in introducing me to Julia. I believe she is the God Dot in my life connecting me to the most beautiful example of loving and letting go. Someday, she might be the one helping me if I ever have to say to my beloved Charlie, "It's okay to go."

Julia was finally able to bring Jay home, but not how she had ever imagined. He had been her college sweetheart whom friends nicknamed "Catbird" for all his zaniness. She and Jay had lived a life full of music, dancing, and travel adventures. Now, after thirty years of marriage, Julia would be doing life alone. She now faced the horrible prospect of planning a funeral. Even given the tragic way he died, she couldn't imagine a service full of black-clad mourners, so she planned what she believed Jay would have loved.

A celebration of the very exuberant life of James Young "Jay" Robinson III was held on June 28, 2021, at four in the afternoon—at a brewery. Guests were asked to "Please wear colors, camo, or costumes (no navy or black), and come prepared to sing and dance in true 'Catbird' fashion." Hundreds of friends, family, and colleagues packed the brewery to remember the man who loved life.

The following year was a blur, as Julia tried to cope without her soulmate. She says now, "I thought I was facing my loss, but really I was just hiding."

When it came time to mark the one-year anniversary of his death, Julia, Sloan, Coleman, and several of Jay's friends and business partners vowed not just to mourn Jay but to commemorate the joyous way he lived life. They decided to create a "Live Like Jay" campaign to celebrate his remarkable fifty-six years. From

April 1, the day of his accident, until June 16, the day of his death, his friends and family pledged to bring love and joy wherever they could. Everyone participating remembered Jay with small acts of kindness for seventy-seven days—the exact length of time he fought to live.

Julia hopes to continue this seventy-seven-day practice every year. "I will always have a hole in my heart and life," she said. "But I am so happy our children know what true love is and how to love and respect another person."

18

Molly, Lucy, Ellie, and Jackie: Room for All

One thing I have learned over and over again is that it can take a lot of time to see whispers come to fruition and see how the God Dots connect. Just as the God Dots in Julia's story took several years to come together, it took nearly two years for all the connections between twin sisters Lucy and Ellie, Molly Painter, and the Team Raleigh crew to unfold. But that multifaceted story was far from over. As Molly and I became friends, I learned the backstory of her whisper to do something about homelessness, which ended up revealing even more divine connections.

Molly grew up in Raleigh in a service-minded family. Her father was a doctor, and both her parents were very involved in the community. "From a very early age I would volunteer with my parents and my brother," she said. She cared not only about giving time but also about creating friendships. "It was the personal relationships that I really enjoyed," she said. "I don't think I realized that until later."

One significant person who shaped Molly's views about leadership and service was her mother, Bonnie Woodruff. While her mom had an inspiring story about making a difference, it was forged out of a family tragedy. Molly's only brother, Ben, was twenty years old when he died in a horrific fire on Mother's Day weekend. Ben had spent the night at the Phi Gamma Delta fraternity house after a graduation party at UNC-Chapel Hill.

"He wasn't even supposed to be there," Molly told me. "But he didn't show up for church the next day or for our family Mother's Day lunch."

Ben Woodruff was one of five students who died of smoke inhalation in the fraternity house that night. It was the deadliest fire in Chapel Hill history. "When my brother died, my mom said she remembers sitting in church asking the Lord to help give her something positive to focus on," Molly said.

Shortly afterward, Bonnie got involved with two projects, one at a children's home and the other campaigning for fire safety on college campuses. She spent years traveling across the country advocating for stricter sprinkler safety laws so that no other mothers would lose their sons or daughters to preventable house fires.

"I watched my mom turn something tragic like that into something that would help others," Molly said.

She was only twenty-three when her brother died, and it permanently affected how she saw the world. "I think when you go through something like that you mature quicker, and you ask yourself, 'What am I really doing with my life?'"

At the time, Molly was working in the fashion industry in New York, and she ended up marrying her college boyfriend, Michael Painter. They moved back to North Carolina for Michael's job with a financial firm. She worked as an interior designer, became a mom to three daughters, and continued to volunteer. She wanted to give back in ways she could create relationships, not just donate money.

"When I was working on a Habitat house for our church, I ended up befriending the family who would live there, and we are still friends," Molly said. "I wanted that connection. It didn't feel like giving to me unless I had created a personal connection."

Her friend Katie Koon asked if she would be interested in helping at the women's shelter in Raleigh, and Molly was hooked once she began creating those connections. At first, the volunteer opportunity was designed as a summer Bible study program, but Molly, Katie, and their friends quickly realized that was not what was wanted or needed. "The women just wanted to talk," Molly said.

It is such a basic human desire to want to belong, and the women in the shelter were no different. They craved community and connection. Molly and her friends decided to make the program more like a coffee shop than a formal Bible discussion. She said it was like they started their own version of a Starbucks in the women's shelter.

"Katie would wear her little barista apron, and we would make them mochas," Molly said. "She got to know everyone's drink order!"

Over those coffee drinks, Molly and her friends also got to know the women and their stories. Hearing about their daily struggles on the street and seeing them with wet blankets and clothing after a rainy night broke Molly's heart. "My whisper was becoming so strong. We had to *do something*, and it wasn't going to go away until I did."

It was in these coffee sessions that she became friends with Ellie, Lucy's twin. Ellie became one of the most important personal connections prompting Molly to believe she needed to do something more about housing. At the time, Ellie herself was coming to terms with her life and what had happened to bring her from being a state high school soccer star to, as she described herself, "a homeless vagrant."

"That was the hardest part to admit to myself. I was almost forty-five years old with no bank account, no address, and a long record of petty theft to survive on the streets," Ellie said.

Like so many other women in Raleigh, she was sleeping at night behind the women's center with a blanket and a makeshift mattress. "If you don't have housing, it is impossible to succeed," she said. "Even birds have nests, and animals have a den, but if you don't have that as a human, you will never feel safe."

As Molly got to know Ellie and understood her daily challenges living on the street, she knew she needed to find a way to do more—just like Julia Robinson and her Prayers in the Park group. Molly and her friends began driving the women to the grocery store, helping them move into apartments if they found housing, and advocating for them to get into available programs.

Ellie admits that even if you were clean and sober, housing was impossible to find. "You had to become wily like a coyote, finding a garage or old shed to sleep in and hoping you didn't get shot by a homeowner," she said. "There were so many times I thought I would not survive the night, but God was looking out for me."

As Ellie put her name on waiting lists for programs and housing, so did many others. She said there was a saying among women on the streets in Raleigh. "You won't go hungry and you won't lack for hygiene, but you won't find housing!"

When Molly read *The Hundred Story Home*, with the explanation of how we created a Housing First program that provided case management along with a home, she found an answer to her whisper.

"I was on the beach, and I was by myself reading your book," Molly told me. "I was sitting there weeping because I knew we had to do this, and I didn't know how we were going to do it in Raleigh. But there was no way to ignore it. Really it wasn't a whisper, it was a loud, clanging gong."

That is when Molly emailed asking about a tour of Moore Place. The same tour where I assumed at first that Molly and her friends were a "drive-by" book club. The same tour where I realized the God Dots were connecting us all to Lucy and Ellie.

After our tour, Molly knew this was her whisper. "For me, Moore Place was always the model," she said.

To trust that whisper, however, was going to take a lot of money and a lot of perseverance. Molly and her friends began talking with anyone who would listen about creating permanent supportive housing in Raleigh. One of their calls was to CASA, an organization that had been building affordable housing for families, veterans, and seniors for more than three decades.

Even at their first meeting with the CASA representatives, Molly said, "I felt like we had a real heart connection for all the same people who kept falling through the cracks in the system."

CASA had just purchased six acres for a new affordable housing project, but they had not yet finalized plans. Over a series of meetings, Molly kept encouraging a partnership that could serve chronically homeless women like Ellie and others they helped at the women's center.

Together they created a powerful private-public partnership, and she was invited to lead the capital campaign to raise the funds needed to build housing on the newly purchased land. They named it King's Ridge in memory of Deborah King, who had been the CEO of CASA for over twenty-three years but had recently passed away from cancer. King's Ridge would become one hundred apartments that would serve families and individuals experiencing homelessness.

CASA's track record of housing experience and Molly's personal passion were a winning combination. One of the first gifts to the campaign came from Molly's own church, St. Michael's Episcopal, and that $50,000 donation was the beginning of many for King's Ridge. She recruited others, calling on family and friends to join the campaign.

"When I look back on it all, it was overwhelming and complicated at times, but it wasn't hard," she said. "It just felt right."

At the same time she was raising money to build King's Ridge, Molly was still volunteering, and one of her favorite outings was with Ellie. They walked every week since Ellie had been accepted into a new temporary transitional housing program in Raleigh.

Lucy and Ellie were now firmly reconnected as well. "It was like we were best friends again in tenth grade!" Ellie said. "We came together again so easily because Lucy made it so easy."

Having family again was a huge motivator for her. She knew she needed to finally address her mental health issues and ask for help. "I had reached a point where I didn't recognize myself anymore. I felt like Tom Hanks in the movie *Cast Away*!" Ellie said. "I would look in the mirror and ask myself, 'How did you become this?'"

Reuniting with Lucy made Ellie want to succeed for herself and her sister. "I wanted to make my family proud of me again," she said. "I can't even put into words how generous and accepting Lucy, Greg, and their children were with me."

Lucy shopped with Ellie, helping her with necessities, clothing, and even a new mattress. "You can't believe how wonderful it is to have a mattress!" Ellie said. "I told Lucy that if I win the Powerball lottery, I am giving half to her and Greg to try to pay them back for all they have done!"

When she moved into the short-term housing program, it was into a room in a home that still needed furniture. Molly Painter had been helping furnish the home, and she called Jackie Craig to see if Green Chair had any twin-size beds that might fit the small bedrooms. Jackie told Molly they didn't often have adult beds, but she had a wooden twin-size headboard and frame she would be willing to donate personally. That bed turned out to be truly the perfect God Dot connection.

What Ellie didn't know until much later was that the bed once belonged to Jackie Craig's mom. She had recently passed away, and Jackie wanted her mother's furnishings to be lovingly recycled, just like all the thousands of items Jackie had helped find new homes for over the years.

Today, Ellie, who finally reunited with Lucy because of a whisper, sleeps each night in a bed because Jackie Craig followed her whisper. And soon dozens of women like Ellie will finally find a home because Molly Painter trusted her own whisper.

After raising over $26.4 million, King's Ridge will begin accepting tenants in 2024. Molly said, "I see God in it every step of the way. Even when we don't know the next step, God keeps putting down the next stone, and we just need to step."

After years of trusting her whispers, Jackie Craig agrees. "I know it is hard to live in the gray and move into the unknown without knowing the outcome," she said. "But I have seen over and over again that when you give up the known for the unknown, that is when the magic happens."

19

Lydia, Lucy, and Ellie: An Angel Donation

Over the next few years, the God Dots between Jackie, Molly, Ellie, and Lucy continued to connect. When Ellie received an honorary certificate upon graduating from her transitional housing program, both Molly and Lucy were there to celebrate. Molly successfully completed her capital campaign to build King's Ridge, raising over $26.4 million to help house individuals and families experiencing homelessness. Since Ellie was already housed in a transitional program, she would not be eligible for a home in King's Ridge, but there was one last divine connection in her story still to be discovered.

It began when Jackie Craig texted me about her friend Lydia Reese. They had met recently for breakfast, and Jackie brought Lydia a copy of *The Last Ordinary Hour*. Jackie knew she had been going through some medical issues with her granddaughter, Olivia, and thought the book's theme of living with medical uncertainty might resonate. As Jackie listened, Lydia described the medical nightmare her family had been experiencing with her seven-year-old granddaughter, the only child of her daughter, Carrie, and Carrie's husband, Jack.

Always a sweet, loving child, at age five, Olivia suddenly began having violent tantrums, unable to eat or sleep.

"It was like a switch flipped," Lydia said.

At the time, she and her husband, Sam, were renting a house across the street from their daughter's family because their own home in a condominium development had been damaged during a major fire in downtown Raleigh. The fire had started at an apartment complex under construction and caused smoke and water damage in nine other buildings. Lydia and Sam had been displaced for over a year, but it turned out to be a blessing to be so near their granddaughter. Taking care of Olivia had become a full-time job for the whole family. Her symptoms were so severe that there were times when the precious little girl had to be restrained from hurting herself and others.

"It's hard to imagine how scary it was," Lydia said. "At five years old, Olivia had suicidal thoughts. She even asked her parents to hide the knives because she was afraid of what she might do."

Both she and her daughter, Carrie, knew this was not normal for any child, and especially not Olivia. Carrie began researching every possible diagnosis, looking for answers. Eventually, Olivia was diagnosed with PANS—just like Lucy Fields' son, Jacob, and Liz Clasen-Kelly's son, Isaac.

As Lydia was telling all this to Jackie Craig, Jackie remembered I'd told her about the amazing God Dot connection between Liz and Lucy and their sons. Jackie offered to connect Lydia with me so that I could introduce her to Lucy.

Once connected, Lucy Fields and Lydia Reese became dear friends bonded by their shared understanding of this devastating, rare disease.

"People can't comprehend what it's like living with a child with PANS," Lydia said. "These kids are remarkably strong, and they can sometimes pull things together when others are around, but for their families, it's terrifying. Children act out in unbelievable ways because their brains are just hijacked."

Lydia and Lucy had a shared understanding of how difficult the tantrums, anxieties, depression, and insomnia are for children with PANS. The disease seems to happen out of the blue, and families are left reeling.

"It was so great to talk to Lucy because she was someone on the other side of it all who could offer some hope," Lydia said. "She became a beautiful resource in my life."

When Lydia and Lucy met, Olivia was seven years old and was already seeing the same doctor who treated both Jacob and Isaac, Dr. Trifiletti in New Jersey. He determined she had PANDAS, which is a small subset of PANS in which each infection or "flare" is associated with a streptococcal infection, specifically the one that causes strep throat.

"Dr. Trifiletti said Olivia had a very severe case of PANDAS," Lydia said. "For such a little girl, she was very sick."

Olivia underwent one round of the treatment for PANDAS through Intravenous Immunoglobulin (IVIG) therapy in New Jersey, and then had six more rounds at home in Raleigh.

While Olivia was receiving treatment, another God Dot connection was forming between Lucy and Lydia. Even though they talked and emailed all the time, they had never met in person or discussed other personal details about their lives. Lucy had no idea that Lydia and Sam had started a family foundation in Raleigh that focused on homelessness and had already been a major contributor to Molly Painter's whisper, King's Ridge. While her own struggle was in the rearview mirror, Lydia's past gave her great empathy for women struggling with addiction and homelessness.

Lydia grew up in what she described as a dysfunctional family. "My mom was bipolar and had several suicide attempts," she said. "I was the oldest of three, so a lot fell on me."

She met the guy who would become her husband while she was still in middle school. She was two years older than Sam when they began dating in high school, but she ended up leaving home as soon as she graduated. The couple moved in together before getting married three days after Sam turned eighteen, but it was a tough few years as they each worked jobs during the day in order to attend NC State classes at night. While Lydia completed accounting classes, she never graduated, and neither did Sam. Both struggled with addictions that took years of Narcotics Anonymous and Alcoholics Anonymous to work through. Along the way, they became parents to two children and even divorced once but then remarried.

In 1995, Sam and Lydia started a company together that grew to employ over two hundred employees and two hundred subcontractors. With the profits from their successful business, they decided to start a foundation to serve others who struggled with addiction and homelessness. "I wanted to give back, and I had always volunteered," Lydia said. "I just think that is the way God intended us to live—to be there for each other."

Due to her own battle, she had a heart for women suffering from addiction, and she helped start a Narcotics Anonymous program at the women's state prison. She also helped organize medical mission trips to Haiti, coordinating doctors and nurses who could assist in the poorest areas. "Some of the people we saw walked for hours to reach our clinic," she said.

While she was familiar with both medical hardship and life challenges before her granddaughter became sick, PANS was a different kind of struggle. "It was a whole different kind of desperate you can't fix," she said.

By the time Lydia and I met, Olivia had been suffering from PANS/PANDAS and its residual symptoms for almost four years. It was no longer a day-to-day battle, but Olivia still had ongoing anxiety and lasting OCD behaviors. At the peak of her illness, she lost 10 percent of her body weight because she could not eat, and she could not sleep at night because she was plagued with irrational fears. The lasting healing that Lydia prayed her granddaughter would find did not seem to come. While she continued to care for Olivia, Lydia kept engaged in the volunteer work and the foundation, which allowed her to focus on things she could help fix.

· · · ·

Lydia had met Linda Nunnallee twenty-five years before, during a Monday night Bible study at their church. Since that time, Linda had become the executive director of StepUp Ministry in Raleigh, a nonprofit providing jobs, life skills, and stability for adults. Lydia understood the ministry's mission. Her own long journey to becoming financially independent had started after she moved away from home at only age eighteen.

Linda told her that StepUp was partnering with a new nonprofit that offered a yearlong transitional housing program for women. This new partner program was looking to open a second home to expand options for housing beyond just one year. Lydia was intrigued, so Linda set up a meeting with the director of the new pilot housing program, who told her all about two residents they were serving.

"They had two women who were completing the one-year program and needed more time," Lydia told me. "I just felt called to help." While Lydia did not meet the two women who would receive the additional housing, she asked that her donation be used to house them.

It would be almost a year after she made that donation that Lydia would find out who her donation had been helping.

Lucy Fields was still helping families with PANS and grateful to be reunited with her twin sister. Ellie had been housed for almost two years through different assistance programs in Raleigh, and she had even been able to work part-time jobs. But one morning, Lucy was devastated to receive a phone call that Ellie was going to lose her housing at the end of the year. The director of the program told Lucy that Ellie had not done anything wrong, but the program was going to be phased out due to lack of funding. The director mentioned that she was calling two other people to tell them the news, because each of them had been huge supporters of the program. One of the names did not surprise Lucy: Molly Painter. Molly had continued helping Ellie and other women as she worked to build King's Ridge. But the other name was a complete surprise: Lydia Reese.

"I couldn't believe it," Lucy told me. "Here we'd been talking for almost a year and a half but only about PANS, so we'd never talked about Ellie."

Lydia had no idea that Lucy had a twin sister. Lucy had no idea Lydia had written a large check only months before to help fund the very housing program that was helping Ellie. Connecting those God Dots was profound for both Lucy and Lydia.

"I did not know Ellie was her sister," Lydia told me. "Definitely God at work here."

Lucy could not agree more, and she sent me a text about the aha moment when she realized Lydia had unknowingly been helping her sister.

It's another huge reminder that we're all connected, and Spirit/God has got this!

Lydia and Lucy teamed up to persuade the program to use Lydia's original donation to extend Ellie's housing and keep her from becoming homeless again. The nonprofit agreed that they would keep Ellie housed for at least one more year so she could save up money and find a new housing solution.

Lucy and I were on a walk in Charlotte, catching up, when she explained this whole story, connecting all the God Dots for me. When Lucy told me that Lydia was the angel donor behind it all, I stopped on the sidewalk and stared at her in disbelief.

"You mean you and Lydia knew each other for a year and a half, but you never knew until that moment that Lydia was helping Ellie, and she didn't know that you were her twin sister?" I asked.

"Yes! Crazy, right?" Lucy said. "It's just unbelievable!"

We walked a little farther, talking about how well Ellie was doing.

"She's come so far," Lucy said. "She's even working part-time at a boarding place for dogs."

At this point, it was Lucy's turn to stop walking, and she said, "I almost forgot! That is the other unbelievable part of this story! You remember Linda Nunnallee is the executive director of StepUp?"

I nodded, not sure where she was going with the story.

"When Ellie started the StepUp program, she recognized Linda, but Linda didn't recognize Ellie," Lucy said. "Ellie was too embarrassed to tell her, but we used to babysit Linda's two children!"

That felt beyond coincidence or serendipity. As young girls, Lucy and Ellie took care of Linda Nunnallee's children, and now Linda headed the StepUp Ministry program that had eventually helped Ellie out of homelessness.

• • • •

When Ellie recounts her years on the streets, she still can't believe how far she fell or how far she has come. "It is exhausting being homeless. Like running a twenty-mile race every day to survive with nowhere to sleep and nowhere to keep your things," Ellie said. "Now I have a car, a bank account, a good credit score, and a part-time job!"

It didn't come easily, and she takes none of it for granted. "I have had so much help from so many good people," she said. "But it all started with housing."

Lucy remains in awe of finding Ellie again after so many years and of all the extraordinary stories of ordinary grace that connect them. "I think the most beautiful and surprising part of finding Ellie is how quickly we formed that same unbreakable bond we'd had as kids. We still spoke our own language without having to say a word," she said. "Even though we've lived vastly different lives from age twenty-one on, we're still each other's person."

Lydia continues to give back through her family foundation and remains hopeful about life for Olivia after PANS. "My greatest hope in this life is that my precious granddaughter will be 100 percent healed. I know that she was created by our loving God, and he makes no mistakes," she said. "I choose to trust that in his time and in his way, she will be healed and will live life abundantly. I am enjoying seeing how God continues to connect beautiful dots in our lives."

20

Caroline: Mountain People

Lydia's love for her family and her hope for healing was a similar theme in another whisper story, but this one had an even more complicated form of healing. When Caroline Hart told me about her whisper to help children, I thought she meant in her professional role, but she meant something much closer to home.

When she and I spoke about it, Caroline was the chief advancement officer of Crossnore Communities for Children. We knew each other because Crossnore is located in the mountains near Charlotte where Charlie and I would go to escape the summer heat. Founded in 1913, Crossnore was created by a physician and her husband who were concerned about kids and education in this very poor Appalachian community. Over the years, Crossnore expanded to several campuses in North Carolina, serving children in the child welfare and foster care system.

When Caroline was younger, foster care and adoption were not subjects she ever knew about or thought she might. She grew up in the small community of Norwood, North Carolina. Even though her parents divorced when she was an infant, she had a happy childhood raised by a loving stepfather who married her mother when Caroline was four. The only adopted kids she knew were a set of three siblings who went to her school and church youth group.

"I remember they were different, but I can't say I understood then why that was," Caroline said. Her mother had very definitive ideas about adoption, and she distinctly remembered her mother saying, "I don't know any adopted children who aren't troubled." She wondered exactly what that meant, but her mother's words stuck with her.

After high school, Caroline went to the all-female Peace College in Raleigh, thinking she would become a schoolteacher. She worked in admissions and led tours for donors and prospective students. After graduation, she continued to work for Peace College and caught the attention of the new incoming female president, who encouraged Caroline to try fundraising and development.

"But I couldn't even sell Girl Scout cookies!" she told her.

The new president kept encouraging her, and Caroline ended up working for Peace for eight years after she graduated. It was during this time that she met Jim Hart, an executive chef hired for a dinner for the college president. Jim had met with Caroline to plan the dinner, but she had no interest in the young chef.

"He was so dirty!" she said. "His jacket, his shoes, even his fingers were always stained with food."

But when he asked her out, a colleague convinced Caroline to accept by telling her, "At least you know you will get a good meal!" She reluctantly agreed, and was shocked when Jim arrived to pick her up in pressed khakis and a button-down shirt. "He cleaned up really well!" Caroline laughed.

After a year and a half of dating, Caroline and Jim were married. By the next year, their first son was born and named McRae, a family name on Caroline's side. Over the next few years, they tried to expand their family but suffered two miscarriages. It had been easy to get pregnant with McRae, and she was devastated to lose two pregnancies, especially one after the first trimester. After the second miscarriage, Caroline was never able to get pregnant again, but doctors could not find a reason why.

She and Jim discussed adoption, but she kept hearing her mother's words about adopted children being "troubled." Caroline focused on her career and was interested when a position opened at Lees-McRae College in Banner Elk, North Carolina, but Jim's first reaction was a hard no.

"We are beach people, not mountain people," he told her. But after a weekend visit, they fell in love with the area and moved to the mountains anyway. The move also changed Jim's career, and he went to seminary. Jim loved being a lifelong learner, but Caroline never imagined she would become a "preacher's wife." At first, Jim wasn't sure he wanted to be a lead pastor, but it turned out he was a wonderful storyteller who could tell a great sermon. Jim was also a gifted couples' counselor, so what began as a part-time job grew into a full-time ministry.

Caroline had been at Lees-McRae for four years when a search firm contacted her about a job at Crossnore. "I told them I wasn't interested," she said.

But the new executive director, Brett Loftis, wasn't taking no for an answer. He drove two different times to Banner Elk and invited her to tour the campus. "I didn't even know Crossnore existed," Caroline said. "I told Brett I didn't know anything about the child welfare system, but he told me I didn't have to—I just needed to know how to fundraise." However, it was Brett's passion for the children he was helping that finally convinced her to take the job.

Caroline began working at Crossnore in 2014, and she quickly realized how much she had to learn. The campus was an incredible sanctuary designed for children who had come from some of the toughest homes filled with neglect and abuse. Crossnore was known for keeping sibling groups together in cottage-style homes with staff members who served as "cottage parents." Children went to school on the tree-filled campus with acres of green grass, playgrounds, and even therapy dogs roaming around. But as beautiful as it all was, Caroline went to Brett after only two weeks and tried to quit.

"I don't think I can do this," she told him. "I go home every night crying!"

In those two weeks, Caroline had started to understand the type of children Crossnore served and why they'd been removed from their parents. Some had been locked in closets. Others were abandoned and beaten. Some had parents who were heroin addicts.

"I thought those things only happened in the movies," she told Brett. But Brett convinced her to reframe her thinking. It wasn't about what they *couldn't do* for children before they came to Crossnore. Their work was about what they *could do* once the children walked in their doors.

"That changed everything for me," Caroline said. "I went home and thought about how much I could raise in order to give all those kids everything we give to our own son, McRae." It was a huge motivator, and she began to love her role.

When she had been at Crossnore a little over two years, a sibling set of four children arrived. There were three brothers and a sister: Cain (nine), Aiden (eight), Nevaeh (six), and Liam (four). The three younger children had been found in a car next to a convenience store dumpster near the highway. For several days, Aiden, Nevaeh, and Liam had been seen by the store clerk coming in and out of the store, stealing food. When the clerk followed them outside to investigate, he found they were living in the car, and their mother was unconscious in the front seat, surrounded by heroin and needles. A member of the Department of Social Services found Cain at a mobile home by himself and brought all four children to Crossnore.

It had not been the first time DSS had received a call on these children. All told, there were twenty-six complaints from several different counties, as the parents had moved the family around to escape authorities. Caroline remembers reading one of the reports, which described "a naked toddler in the street." That one was about baby Liam playing in the road with a dead squirrel.

Even for Crossnore, the children were difficult to handle. They had been unparented all their lives with a father cycling in and out of jail and a mother who was a heroin addict.

"They were more like wild animals," Caroline admitted. "They'd had to steal food to survive, and their mom would even lock them outside in the mornings. Sometimes they weren't let back inside the home at night, so they built a fort and slept in the woods."

All four children were kept together in one of the Crossnore cottages and began adjusting to life in their new home, which included attending church on Sundays—and Jim happened to be the pastor. Caroline noticed Nevaeh watching her and McRae during services. "McRae would sit next to me in the pew with his head on my shoulder, and Nevaeh would just stare at us," she said.

At first, Caroline didn't fully understand that Nevaeh had come to Crossnore with three brothers. Because that little girl was pulling on her heartstrings, she asked one of the Crossnore case managers about her. That is when Caroline discovered they were a sibling set of four. The case manager explained they were still in line for reunification, meaning the courts were working with the parents to take them back. But the parents had not shown up to court the last three times, so it was more likely the children were headed for adoption.

"Can you imagine adopting four children?" Caroline said to Jim when she found out precious Nevaeh had three brothers.

While she wasn't looking to adopt one child, much less four, Nevaeh still tugged at her heart. Caroline even learned the young girl's name was "heaven" spelled backward.

Jim and Caroline decided they could at least help a little more by becoming mentors for the four children, so they began taking them on outings with McRae. As an only child, McRae didn't mind having company and got along especially well with the oldest boy, Cain. In December 2016, the Harts invited the four children to make Christmas cookies at their home. Liam crawled up onto Caroline's lap and said, "I wish you were my mommy."

It was endearing but still not a possibility. Everyone knew re-unification was still possible for the four kids. But as more time passed, the parents still had not improved. They made promises to their children but never followed through. They scheduled visits but never showed up. Worst of all, they never appeared for man-dated court dates. By that spring, the case managers, lawyers, and judges were fed up. The children would be placed into the adoption system. Since Jim and Caroline had grown close with the children, they had to help explain to them what was happening.

"What does it mean to be adopted?" Cain asked Caroline, and it was an impossible question to answer. To make it even more difficult, they would have to explain it was unlikely the children would be kept together. As the youngest, Nevaeh and Liam might stay together, but Cain and Aiden were less likely to find a "forever home" since people generally chose younger children to adopt. In that case, the older boys would stay in the Crossnore cottage home until they were of age to live alone. The future for all four children looked very uncertain given their extensive trauma and how far below grade level they all were, having missed so much school.

Even though she wanted to help them, Caroline knew that, as a group, they were overwhelming. The Hart family of three was very easy, with McRae heading into high school, and it seemed impossible to take on four more children.

But in April 2017, four months after baking Christmas cookies with the kids, Caroline was flying to Dallas when she began reading *The Hundred Story Home* on the plane. When she got to the last chapter in the book, titled "Trust the Whisper," she began weeping.

"I remember putting the book down on my lap, and tears were just running down my face," she told me later.

Caroline had a whisper. She knew it. She had just not wanted to listen. It was too overwhelming to imagine. But finally, that whisper was just too insistent to ignore. "When I got off the plane,

I called Jim," she said. "I told him we had to do something about these kids."

Jim told her he'd been hearing the same whisper for a while. He just didn't know what she would think.

"It was such a relief!" Caroline told me. "I knew that when I got back from Dallas, we were going to do more. We just weren't quite sure what that was."

Caroline and Jim still didn't imagine it was going to be adoption, just something more like foster care. They tried some overnights with all four kids, and then they took Liam on a beach weekend. Nevaeh, Aiden, and Cain were going on a Crossnore field trip to the ocean, but Liam was too young to go with the bigger group. So they took McRae, Liam, and another Crossnore teen to the beach—and Caroline said that sealed the deal.

"Liam had never had anyone hug and love him," she said. "After that weekend, I just knew somehow he was going to be our kid."

Caroline and Jim began training to become foster parents, thinking that was their next step, but when the children's birth parents failed to show that July for yet another court date, the judge moved to terminate their parental rights. The final court date was set for three months away, October 2017.

"I think that is when we realized this was not going to be a foster situation," Caroline said. "These children were about to become ours."

Over the next month, nothing about the decision was easy. Nevaeh, Liam, Aiden, and Cain began living with the Hart family— and all four children began acting out.

"They were coming to grips with the fact that their parents had abandoned them," Caroline said. "There was so much anger. So much hurt."

There was bedwetting and screaming and punching holes in the walls, not because they didn't want to be adopted but because they didn't want to believe they had been abandoned. These children, who had never been loved or disciplined, became once again the wild animals they'd been raised to be.

To the outside world, Jim and Caroline looked like adoring parents who were giving a new home to four orphans, but inside their home it was a disaster.

"It was beginning to look like we couldn't do it," she admitted. "It was destroying our marriage and destroying our home."

When the next court date arrived, they stood before the judge when he asked, "Are you prepared to adopt these children?" Despite all the chaos of the past few months, they said that they were. The judge told them, "Congratulations! We need more people like you."

Over the next two years, all seven of them would go to therapy, and Jim and Caroline would go to couples therapy. "We had four traumatized children, and everyone went backward before we went forward," Caroline admitted.

At different times, each of the children tested the boundaries and love of their new parents, trying to see if they would give up. They didn't. They came together to heal as much as they could for these kids, and there was a lot to heal. All the children's teeth were rotten; Liam had been given mostly Mountain Dew in his baby bottles. Everyone was far behind in school; Aiden had severe ADHD, and his father had tried to beat it out of him, knocking out his front teeth in the process. There were both mental scars and physical scars, but Caroline learned to take one day at a time.

"They had never made lists for Santa or had an Easter basket," she said. So they began to make new memories together and created new family traditions.

McRae might have had the biggest adjustment to make, as four loud and unruly children moved into their quiet little family. When Caroline and Jim were training to become foster parents, McRae had to be interviewed as well. He told the interviewer, "I have had a good childhood with good parents. It would be really selfish of me not to share them with someone else."

• • • •

Caroline knows not everyone is in a position to adopt one child, much less four, but she believes we can all do something to help. "I want people to understand that there are children who are hurting, and it is not their fault. The system is broken."

It is a complicated system to fix, but children caught in that system can be healed.

McRae is now in college, Cain and Aiden are in high school, and Nevaeh and Liam are in middle school. They are all on grade level, and Caroline thinks they are about "as normal as a family of seven can be." Her whisper to adopt four children obviously saved their young lives, but I asked her what she thought it had done for her own life. She teared up before answering.

"It's what I was always supposed to do and be," she said. "It's funny; Jim and I didn't want to move to the mountains because we thought we were beach people. But this is why we had to move to the mountains—we had to meet our kids."

21

Livvi: Longing for Home

As I was hearing the stories of people working for good and listening to quiet callings, like Caroline Hart, I realized how many were connected to my own whisper to *Write it down*. When I first started listening to that whisper and writing, it felt ridiculous. I could not believe anyone was ever going to want to read my books.

When I began meeting people like Caroline Bundy, with her teen shelter whisper, and Molly Painter, with her housing whisper, I knew I wasn't alone in listening. More importantly, my listening was connecting me to people and stories I never would have known. I never imagined, however, that one day I would receive an email from a woman thousands of miles away named Livvi, who found the courage to embark on her own whisper.

Livvi's email was written late at night the day after Christmas 2022, and I opened it the following day. As usual, I'd woken up early, hoping to catch a glimpse of the sunrise before settling in to do some writing. Usually I try not to be distracted by emails, but I remember reading Livvi's first and last name in my inbox. When I realized I didn't recognize her name, I became curious, especially when I noted the time it was sent: 10:44 p.m. I was sure Livvi had no idea that certain numbers mattered to me, but I had started paying extra attention to anything with the numbers eleven and forty-four; I'd noticed those divine patterns often led to a God Dot connection.

When I first opened her email, I almost laughed out loud. Livvi's opening line was:

I found your book in a discount store in Michigan.

No author wants to read that their hard work was now collecting dust in a bargain bin bookstore with a price tag so low the retailer is practically giving away copies. But Livvi's second sentence stopped me from laughing.

Immediately I knew this was going to be a different kind of email from a reader. Here is Livvi's message exactly as it was written to me:

I found your book in a discount store in Michigan. And it took up weight and space and I didn't touch it until I was sitting under a bridge by the train tracks in Florida. Waiting days for a train to the next town. I ended up finishing your book just a day or two later in my sleeping bag behind a walmart in that next town. I've been houseless since I was 17, and I've been traveling around the country mostly on foot since I was 18. I'm 23 now, and up until a year ago it never bothered me. I loved looking up at the stars and listening to traffic or water rush by me. I loved being somewhere new every couple nights. I still do. But about a year ago I started to feel something stir in me. I started feeling tired. The backpack is heavy and the walks are long. You stop looking like a kid, and it feels like people don't care how well you play or sing, they want to help you less and less. In the discount store in Michigan I picked up quite a few books and read the backs. Nothing really caught my eye. But before I even read the back of The Hundred Story Home I just felt that it had to come with me. I had heard about the housing first movement but I didn't know much about it until now. I've known I've wanted to settle down and live an easier life for a while now, but I didn't know how.

The Hundred Story Home brought me to tears for many reasons. The first is that "oh my God, there really are people who care. People who see me and my friends and want to do something about it." The joy that came with hearing these stories of people, much like me or others I know, flourishing.

The second, is I realized how much I longed for a space to call my own. Somewhere I can relax and not worry about being woken up, or being cold, or wet. The ability to do things without carrying a 40lb pack. Go to therapy and get treatment for my mental and physical illnesses.

The third is the fear that realization instilled in me. There's a certain freedom to this lifestyle, but there are sacrifices too. But I had accepted it and I was happy. The first 4 years I was on the road was the happiest I had ever been, but we're halfway to year 6 and I'm not happy anymore.

I've been offered an apartment all my own through a housing first situation in Spokane. I'm in New Orleans, but I've made the trip before. I'm terrified, honestly. I'm scared that I'll f--k it up. Or that I'm not ready. I'm scared that with the lifestyle change I'll become a different person, and even if it's for the better, it's scary! But I know I need it. I know this will be good for me, and I can travel again someday, but differently.

I might be rambling a little, but I want you to know how what you've done has made a difference in lives of those you haven't even met. You housed the homeless, and not only are you inspiring other people to do the same, you're inspiring homeless from across the country to become housed. It might be small in the grand scheme of all that you've done, but it matters a great deal to me. I currently struggle with the whole God thing, but something told me I had to take the d--n book. And within a week of finishing it, doors opened to opportunity. I've been trying to figure out in my head if emails from the homeless are a common occurrence in your life, I'm certain I can't be the only one to reach out while currently experiencing houselessness. But with lack of access to certain things, I fear that I am. Either way, that same something that told me to buy the book told me to send this email, but as I type it I do feel a bit silly. Regardless, thank you for restoring some of my hope, and happy holidays!

By the time I finished reading, I was crying. Livvi's letter had to be the best God Dot I could ever hope to connect, for so many reasons. First, the book I almost didn't finish writing, for fear no one would read it, had somehow found its way into the hands of a woman at the very moment she needed it.

Second, despite what Livvi imagined, this was the very first time I'd heard from a reader currently experiencing homelessness. It was not a "common occurrence," and Livvi was the first reader who told me I had restored some of her hope.

But what truly took my breath away was our incredible whisper and God Dot connection. For me to be reading this email and crying over it, so many seemingly ordinary moments had aligned in an extraordinary way.

It began with a whisper fifteen years ago to invite Denver Moore to speak at the Roof Above soup kitchen, which led to my new understanding that solving homelessness was not about soup or programs—it was about homes.

That understanding gave me a story to write, even though I thought no one would ever read it. And that led to an insistent whisper for a young woman named Livvi to pick up a book from a bargain bin and read it in her sleeping bag behind Walmart.

And finally, another whisper came to Livvi to send a late-night email to an author she'd never met. Even though she felt silly typing it, she listened.

I read over her email multiple times, taking in all the details. As I read it, I thought about how Livvi considered the "weight and space" of the book in her decision to carry *The Hundred Story Home*. Other than what she'd read on the back cover, Livvi had no idea there would be a message inside that seemed meant only for her—to believe in the power of housing. When she decided to carry my book in her backpack, all Livvi knew was the whisper to take it was insistent. I reread my favorite line from her letter:

> I currently struggle with the whole God thing, but something told me I had to take the d--n book. And within a week of finishing it doors opened to opportunity.

Isn't that just the same for all of us? We struggle with this "whole God thing," but sometimes we get such a strong divine nudge we have to pay attention. When we do, there is usually a door waiting to be opened.

I wrote back to Livvi that morning, wondering if she would ever read my email and how she'd written to me in the first place. I knew many people experiencing homelessness would get internet access at a library. That was probably what she meant when she wrote that she doubted she was the first person experiencing homelessness to write to me, "But with lack of access to certain things, I fear that I am."

While it is not usually difficult for me to write an email, it took me a while to know what to say to Livvi. Finally, I wrote:

> To open my email this morning and read your words brought me to tears, and I am in awe that you found the book and that it followed you (heavy in your backpack) until you finally read it. It also brings me to tears to imagine you in your sleeping bag behind a Walmart reading it. I am honored to know your story.

> That feeling to pick it up, to keep carrying it, to read it, and to write me about that—that's all, in my mind, your whispers. To think this has led you to be open to housing at the same time that help is offered—to me, that is evidence of the divine in the world. You might call it God, or Spirit, or the universe at work. I love that you are now open to receiving help for mental and physical needs and maybe even some trauma from the streets.

> I am so glad you listened to all those whispers. All of that connects us in the most miraculous way—I call it a God Dot connection. Maybe we

are connected so that you would be ready to say yes to help. Maybe we are connected so that you could remind me that my words matter. Because I do forget and, no, I don't get hundreds of emails, just a few special ones like yours.

Maybe we are connected because someday I can help you write your story. We will have to wait and see. But one thing is for sure: you made my day, my month, maybe my year. Thank you for that, and please stay in touch. I would love to know how you are doing, and if you ever write songs I would love to read one of those too.

Thank you again. May you keep following those whispers that lead you to more good things in your life.

Two days later, I heard back from Livvi. She wrote,

Please, call me Levi. It's short for my road name, Leviathan, and I've always liked it more. I've just had this email since I was like 14 years old.

We exchanged a few emails over the winter and spring as she worked her way across the country from New Orleans to Spokane. Each time I opened an email, I hoped it would say she was housed. I told her that her writing was good and encouraged her to write her story someday. This is what she told me:

All of this really does make me believe everything is happening just as it's supposed to. I call it the Universe, but all the same, it is Divine. If I ever write a good song, I'll be sure to send it to you. But honestly, I want to start writing novels again. I'm already writing my feelings down again, and I'm flattered that you say my writing in the email is good. I'm just trying to put good intention and my honest emotions into my words. Maybe one day, I'll actually complete a book of my own. But one step at a time.

I'll definitely keep in touch, and I'll let you know when I get my keys. I would be honored to share that exciting day with you. I'm really grateful for all that you've done, and I'm beyond happy to have made even just your day! Your words matter more than you know, and even when it's hard, I hope you never forget it again. I know your work and your book have been changing lives, and will continue to change lives for as long as you live, as long as The Moore Place stands, as long as this book can be found on any shelf. I think the only way it wouldn't, is if the work was done and houselessness was eradicated. On that day you could know you took a part in that, along with everyone who worked to make sure that there are beds where beds should be.

All told, I exchanged emails with Livvi for six months, hoping to hear that she had finally moved into a home. Her last message to me said that she'd arrived in Spokane and found a job, but was still waiting on housing. After that, I emailed her three more times without ever hearing back from her again.

I knew there were a lot of possible reasons that could be. Maybe Livvi decided not to participate in the Housing First program and was once again sleeping behind a Walmart somewhere. Maybe she was housed and just didn't need to write to me anymore. But what I really hoped had not happened was that housing came too late for her. There are a million dangers every night for a young woman alone on the streets. Had Livvi been raped, murdered, or lost into sex trafficking? I would never know.

* * * *

What Livvi shared with me was nearly a full-circle story, but as much as I want her to have a happy ending, I can't make one up for her. I can only hope and pray, as Livvi wrote, that one day we could say that *"houselessness is eradicated,"* which would mean every Livvi would have a home.

Until then, maybe we all can keep hearing and heeding our whispers, even if it is something as simple as picking up a bargain bin book.

22

Andrea: The Last Connection

From Denver Moore to Livvi and all the God Dots in between, each story I've shared in this book is evidence to me of a greater weave in the world. As I've tried to understand how all the connections might be possible, I read about a concept known as "Indra's net." This is a metaphor used in Buddhism, Hinduism, and yoga philosophy, all of which have similar variations of the same idea: imagining our world as if there is a massive net arching overhead. Where each cord meets another, there is a multifaceted jewel, so as each jewel shines it reflects the light of others. According to the ancient metaphor, we are each like one of those jewels, not only connected by every cord in the net but also shining upon each other.[1]

I like to visualize this image because it gives me the tiniest notion how it might be possible that Liz Clasen-Kelly could connect to Lucy and Ellie, then to their sons with PANS, then to Molly's vision for King's Ridge, then to Jackie's furniture ministry, and finally to Lydia Reese's angel donation. When the world around me feels complicated and disconnected, this beautiful "net" makes me feel as if it is all really so simple and connected.

As I discovered new facets of each whisper that led to a God Dot connection, they were like jewels in a necklace of proof. Each story by itself was a shimmering bead, making a single-story case for God. But when they were strung together, I felt like they formed the most beautiful strand of confirmation of the divine story in which we all play a part.

But would other people see it the same way? As I wrote and researched this book, I wondered, *What could be the last jewel in this necklace of proof?*

Then I lost my childhood best friend, Andrea Dorsey, to cancer. What happened after she died felt like that last unmistakable bead.

She and I met in kindergarten at Western Hills Elementary School in El Paso, Texas. While I have no clear memory of our meeting, I also have no memory of Andrea *not* being in my life. It seems like she is a part of almost every childhood recollection I have. My earliest memory of her is from 1969, at my sixth birthday party. My mom picked the theme of comic book costume party, and Andrea arrived as "Goofy," with long, black, felt ears attached to a headband that flopped against her brown hair. She wore a faded yellow turtleneck with high-water red plaid pants and her brother's hippie leather vest. I vividly remember Andrea laughing as she came in the door, tickled by her own costume.

Her laugh was a staple in my life. When Andrea grinned, it would inevitably turn into a chuckle that morphed into deep giggles, until finally we would both be weeping with laughter.

Andrea could find humor in so much of life, and when she couldn't understand something, she would throw up her hands and announce, "Who knew?"

Who knew?

That was my favorite expression of hers. I think she would be saying that today—*Who knew?* Who knew that a persistent earache could be the warning sign for a cancer that would change everything?

Andrea was the heart and soul of Dorsey's Cards and Gifts, a retail store that was a fixture in El Paso for decades. My mom was Andrea's best customer and often lingered in the back of the store sipping a Mocha Frappuccino as she addressed dozens of greeting cards each week. People came for the cards, but they stayed for the conversation. Andrea knew who was dating whom, who was getting divorced, and who was having a baby often before their actual family members did.

Even though she sold sweet, sentimental cards for a living, she was rarely emotional herself, except with her many rescue dogs. Lord Nelson, her enormous Great Dane, would put his paws on her shoulders and lick her face while she whispered loving baby talk. As for humans, however, Andrea was not one to say, "I love you," even to her dearest friends, much less send an emoji-filled text.

There were three of us who remained friends for over fifty years: myself, Andrea, and our third musketeer, Beth McCombs Gast. Beth and I used to laugh about how Andrea, who was in the business of heartfelt communication, would never actually participate in heartfelt communication herself. Beth and I would send her text messages with rainbows, hearts, and smiley faces just to see if we could get anything cutesy back. But Andrea's messages were simply *yes* with no punctuation or *no* without any further explanation.

When Andrea first started fighting cancer, Beth was living in Portland, Oregon, and I was in Charlotte, so it was difficult to keep up across three time zones. We created a text thread between the three of us, Andrea begrudgingly agreeing to participate in our group messaging. Beth and I began sending daily messages to boost her spirits.

"When you beat this cancer, we are celebrating in Jackson Hole!" I texted, and sent photos of the Grand Teton National Park mountains that Andrea had never visited but were on her bucket list. Beth enthusiastically agreed with a string of colorful emojis and a "100 percent" sign.

We kept up this exchange during the many weeks that Andrea endured surgery, radiation, and chemotherapy at the Mayo Clinic in Scottsdale, Arizona. Miraculously, she came through the treatment, and her oncology team believed she could count on at least ten more years. Even though she was only fifty-eight years old, that felt like a huge win. As promised, the three of us met up for the Fourth of July in Jackson Hole to celebrate her remarkable remission. On the last day, as we sat by a pool sipping fruity drinks and eating guacamole, Andrea announced, "We should make this an annual event!"

But we never got to decide if it should become an annual event. Four weeks after our Jackson reunion, I received a text from Andrea with little explanation and no emojis, just the simplest communication of facts about a growth on her eyelid:

Squamous cell. Not just in my eye. It is
everywhere.

I called as soon as I read it, and Andrea picked up, already crying.

"It's unbelievable," she choked. "It's everywhere. My head. My lungs. My liver. I lit up that scan like a Christmas tree. How could it have spread that fast since July?"

She planned to start treatment again as soon as possible, and I promised to join her older sister, Tina, in helping her through the coming weeks of radiation. I imagined sitting by Andrea's bedside, retelling our middle school and high school stories to distract her from the pain. By the time my plane landed in Phoenix, however, she was already in a coma. It seemed that instead of keeping up her spirits, I would be witnessing Andrea's last breaths.

Who knew?

In all the years we were friends, I could only remember meeting Tina a few times because she was twelve years older than we were. When I arrived at the Mayo Hospital ICU, Tina and I hugged beside Andrea's bedside. She no longer looked like Andrea. Only weeks before, she, Beth, and I rode a tram together to the top of a mountain to celebrate. Now, somehow, she already resembled a corpse. It was an unfathomably fast change.

Doctors told us death would be swift and peaceful, so Tina and I gathered by her bedside to create a ritual with prayers and music. The emaciated figure before us did not seem to have any connection to the laughing girl who had dressed as Goofy for my sixth birthday party.

I remembered how I had learned from Julia Robinson that sometimes the most loving thing we can do is to tell someone, "It's okay to go." I had been so worried it would be Charlie I might soon need to spend last hours with; I had never imagined it would be Andrea.

Tina placed her hands on Andrea's right arm, and I held her left hand. My phone would serve as our church music this morning.

"What would you like to start with?" I asked Tina.

"That one with 'lift you up on angel's wings,'" Tina said. "I think Plácido Domingo sings it."

I found a version, and our morning service began. My phone rested on the pillow near Andrea's head, and together we listened to the famous tenor. Andrea showed no sign that she could hear the song, but her chest kept a slow rhythm—left side up, left side down—feebly moving under her blue hospital gown. Her right lung had already collapsed, so only her left side stubbornly fought to keep going.

Throughout the next four hours we alternated a list of favorite songs, from spiritual music to '80s classics, all while sharing our favorite Andrea stories. Tina and I began to tire, but neither of us wanted to stop in case we might miss the actual moment of Andrea's passing. Early that afternoon the hospital chaplain came in, and Tina explained to me that he had met with Andrea only two days before.

"She had a lot of questions," the chaplain said. "She told me she was really angry with God. But I told her that was good, because you have to believe in a God to be angry with God."

After he spoke with Andrea that day, the chaplain told us that she had said, "You have given me a lot to think about." And then she'd allowed him to pray with her.

"You want to offer one last prayer now?" I asked the chaplain.

The three of us held hands around Andrea's bed, and the chaplain blessed and released her to God.

After he left, Tina and I remained, watching the steady left side up, left side down.

Around 4:00 p.m., a doctor came in, and Tina began discussing Andrea's end-of-life progression that had been going on now for over eight hours. All the medical talk seemed to be disrupting the peace, so Tina and the doctor stepped outside. As they slid the door behind them, I noticed a red light was blinking on the top of Andrea's monitor.

I watched for the slow left side up, left side down of her blue hospital gown. I kept waiting. The red light kept blinking.

Two nurses rushed in and began checking the monitor dials. One stood at the foot of the bed and one at the left side of Andrea's motionless head. I couldn't take my eyes off of her blue hospital gown. It wasn't moving.

I looked up just as the nurses exchanged glances. The one at the foot of the bed checked the wall clock and nodded to her teammate, "Time of death 4:09."

That was it. Time of death: 4:09.

Who knew?

After fifty-eight years and a long day of waiting, Andrea's soul had decided to tiptoe out of the room when no one was paying attention. I reached for my phone and selected "The Blessing." Closing my eyes, I held my friend's now-cold hand one last time as the music began.

The Lord bless you and keep you. Make his face shine upon you.

During the full seven minutes of music and amens, I never opened my eyes as the song washed away my tears. I felt like I was in a thin place, and I wanted to stay where I thought I could feel the last wisp of Andrea leaving the room. The last of her physical presence and the beginning of her invisible presence.

Later, as we gathered Andrea's things and prepared to leave the room, Tina and I each felt we had both lost a sister. Andrea and Tina had been born into the same family, but Andrea and I had chosen each other. For more than fifty years, she had been my chosen sister, and I'd just had the honor to help someone I love leave this world.

* * * *

Andrea had been dead almost nine months when I received a text from her.

Charlie and I had been on a plane, and just as we touched down in Texas, I saw a message on my phone. It was a two-word text message with no emojis:

I have

The white bubble glowed on my screen like an otherworldly angel touch. I stared at the impossible message again and noted the time: 11:22. To me, the numbers were another divine message. If this was from Andrea, she had my full attention.

All around me, people began gathering their suitcases from the overhead bins. Charlie stood up, but I stayed in my seat, eyes locked on the screen, wishing it could be true that I had received a message from my fifty-year friend. How did those two words appear on my phone months after Andrea died? And if she was going to send a message, what did "I have" mean? Andrea had what?

I told myself there were a lot of possible rational explanations. Maybe Tina still had Andrea's phone and had accidentally sent the beginning of a message. Maybe somehow those two words "I have" had been caught in the internet cloud for nine months and just arrived. Maybe someone else now had Andrea's cell number and mistakenly sent the text.

I couldn't decide what to do or what to make of it. But if the soul of my best friend of five decades was going to go to all this trouble to reach me, I should at least respond. So, I wrote her back:

> Andrea—so miss you ♡♡ sending love to thin places.

I pressed send, smiling to myself and knowing that if she was still here on earth, Andrea would have rolled her eyes at my heart emojis.

We still had not exited the plane, so I had my phone on my lap when it came to life with the little gray dots indicating someone was typing back. I felt like God Dots were dancing in my hand. It appeared Andrea was texting from heaven.

I stared at the screen in disbelief, waiting for the message. It had to be someone telling me that it was all a text mistake. But after a few seconds passed, the message appeared:

> G

That's it. Capital letter G and no other words.

I felt a full-body tingle. What did it mean? If someone was typing, why not complete the thought? Why send only the letter G?

I was ready to dismiss the whole thing as some technical glitch when the gray circles started dancing again. This time, however, when the message came through it was in perfect human-texting form.

> Your timing is impeccable—I'm in El Paso. You provided so much joy in her life and empathy in mine.

This new message was clearly from Tina. I waited a moment, and the gray dots danced again. It was another longer message from Tina about Andrea, which had to mean she'd mistakenly typed those two short, cryptic messages on her sister's phone. I was more than a little deflated. I wanted to believe it was Andrea communicating from heaven. I responded to Tina without asking about the first messages of "I have" and "G."

Hours later, however, I still could not shake the idea that those two brief messages were somehow Andrea reaching out to me, making her invisible presence known. I thought about how receiving the message from Meg about my dad had seemed improbable, yet it had happened. Maybe this was another such message from a thin place, or maybe I just was telling myself what I wanted to believe. That is one of the most important things I had learned when connecting the God Dots: there is often so much more to the story, and you have to be willing to find out if there *is* more. I texted Tina, but this time I sent the message directly to her cell phone, not Andrea's old number.

> Did you accidentally type the "I have" on her phone? It was just so odd.

I waited for the dancing dots to appear, but it was over an hour before a response from Tina arrived:

> Really strange. I definitely wasn't messaging you. No recollection of typing that and it doesn't fit the other messages I was sending.

My full-body tingle came back. I sent a screenshot of the conversation from Andrea's phone to show Tina what I was seeing. Then I added my own explanation:

> Maybe that reads:

> I have

> God

> ♡☆

There were, of course, any number of ways to interpret what those words "I have" and "G" meant. But every time I stared at my screen, that is how they read to me. Andrea, who had been so angry with God, was now at peace with God. And just like in her earthly life, she offered little explanation and no emojis, just the simplest communication of facts.

Later that evening, Tina replied, agreeing with my assessment, and then added:

Weird. I was on my way to the cemetery.

I'm with you on the divine.

I read her message several times but didn't understand. What did it mean that Tina was headed to the cemetery? I had to know.

Wow. You were on your way to the cemetery?

Yes!! Wow is right! This is my first trip there since her death and I always went there with her. I am now sure it is the right place for her. . . . Too many coincidences.

There were too many coincidences, which meant it absolutely *was* a God Dot, not chance. Now I knew there was more to the story, so I called Tina, who picked up right away.

"Tina, what do you mean that you were headed to the cemetery?" I asked.

It might have been a strange opening line, but Tina and I were so connected at this point, I figured she wouldn't mind. She didn't, and began telling me her side of the story.

"I have been so conflicted about what to do with Andrea's ashes," she said. "We used to visit our parents, who are buried in the cemetery here, but I just didn't know if that was the right place for Andrea. Driving to the cemetery, I had Andrea's ashes in the car with me and I just needed a sign. That's when your text came in on her phone that you missed her, and you were sending love to thin places. Like I said, it was just impeccable timing."

When I was on that plane touching down in Texas, I had no idea Tina was in El Paso worrying about Andrea's ashes. When I sent the message to Andrea saying I missed her, I did not know Tina was on her way to the cemetery at that exact time and was wishing she had some sign from her. When I sent my love and heart emojis, I truly believed I was just honoring Andrea's memory. I didn't believe my message would actually be received or, more importantly, returned.

"Tina, I can't believe this," I said. "You were driving to the cemetery asking for a sign from Andrea when my message came in?"

"Yes," Tina said. "Literally, I had Andrea's ashes on the front seat of my car, wondering what she would want. When I saw your message, I just knew it was her answering me through you."

Tina sent a screenshot of Andrea's phone, confirming what I saw on my end, and added her own message:

Oddly or not, I find the coincidences comforting and confirmatory—a tapestry linking Andrea and us in death to her final resting site.

I smiled as I read. To both of us, the two unexplainable texts were somehow from Andrea. To me, they were that last jewel in my necklace of proof, confirming the divine story that held us all.

In her life on this earth, Andrea had professed little faith. Yet now this dear friend who had been so unsure of God, even angry with him, had been the one to make me believe absolutely in God. *Who knew?*

• • • •

Andrea and I were powerfully connected in this life, and now, even in death, we would never be disconnected. The gray dots dancing on the screen were just like the God Dot connection Andrea and I shared for fifty years and now will share forever.

These same God Dots connect all of us.

There is a current of grace running through this world. When we allow ourselves to plug in to this divine electricity, we can light up our lives, as well as each other's lives, in powerful and unfathomable ways. God is always listening and always answering. We just need to not be afraid or look away.

We cannot dismiss divine experience while at the same time asking where God is in our lives. When we are open enough and look deep enough, there is more to all of our stories.

The proof of God is all around us, just waiting to be seen.

23

A Divine Weave

While I've lived each of these stories or know the person who did, I still cannot begin to fully explain them. From my very first encounter with Denver Moore to the *Ask her what she does* whisper on a plane to meeting the woman in the yellow pants to the final "G" message from Andrea's phone number, each story has an element of wonder that is difficult to comprehend. Because these happenings all seemed so incredible, I rarely talked about them before I wrote this book. My biggest fear was that I would not be believed.

But when I did share one or two of these stories, I was not met with skepticism. In fact, not only would people react in awe but inevitably would begin a discussion of their own God Dot stories. That is when I began understanding their collective power. I wasn't the only one catching a glimpse of God in my life. Lots of people were having their own divine experiences. Most were just choosing to stay quiet about it. Maybe all of us are too afraid to speak about our whispers and God Dots because we believe they might be dismissed by others as too "woo-woo."

Once I started sharing with just a few people, however, I realized the problem with keeping God secret.

If we do not share when we have a direct experience with God, we limit the possibility that these encounters will have the fullest impact in our lives. All the amazing God Dots between twin sisters Lucy and Ellie, stretching to Jackie Craig's furniture-ministry whisper, Molly Painter's housing whisper, and Lydia Reese's angel donation would have remained unknown if we each had remained silent. We never would have understood the miraculous ways we were all linked if we'd remained afraid to talk about it. The real power of grace only becomes evident when we openly discuss it in order to reveal connections so intricate that we could not possibly design them ourselves.

Instead of dismissing my God Dots, I now actively watch for them. Now I fully believe there are no coincidences. We are not here by accident. Our fates are very much tied to one another. As I was writing these pages, I tried to keep that at the forefront of every chapter. I didn't want to share stories that could be diminished as serendipity, although I have experienced plenty of those as well. I wanted to share stories I believed could only be evidence of God.

For me, it comes down to this: Is it more difficult to believe that all these people in my life and their connections are the result of random, small-world coincidences? Or is it more difficult to accept that we are all connected by a complex, divine web, like the image of Indra's net, which is only visible once we are paying attention? It is like the constellations: once someone shows you the patterns in the stars, you can't *not* see them.

While the signs might be small, the connections between each of us are impossibly, intricately interwoven once we begin to pay attention. There are miracles all around us every day. When we are feeling overwhelmed and unsure how to find our path, we need to be reminded that God is not above us or beyond us but rather right beside us. God is always whispering. We just need to be ready to listen.

Fifteen years ago, I could not fully accept God, angels, signs, or anything I could not logically explain. I thought it had to be science *or* faith—not embracing the realm of *both*. I thought the point of this human experience was defined only by what we could achieve, not by what we came to believe. I refused to see the many signs in my life that suggested otherwise.

The first time I recognized a God Dot in my life was the day I met Denver Moore, but I didn't talk about it. How could I explain that a stranger who had been homeless for thirty years had shaken me awake in such a way that I could never fall back asleep into the life I had before? There was an undeniable aspect of that meeting with him that felt like a divine appointment I was destined to have. Even though it was my most life-changing moment, for a long time I was afraid to talk about it, and many other experiences, because I was worried what people would say about me. I was afraid to admit I'd caught a glimpse of God in my life.

Reverend Lauren Artress, an Episcopal priest at Grace Cathedral in San Francisco, told me, "The church is afraid of direct experience."

Her words struck a chord with me. Meeting Denver was an experience that left me with a certainty I had come alive to something and, as a result, my life was never the same. It was a feeling I'd never experienced in a church. That divine encounter swept me out of my ordinary life and into a world of the extraordinary, one filled with God Dot stories.

I don't think it is only "the church" that is afraid of direct experience. I believe we as people are afraid of divine experience. We are not sure what to do with the holy in our lives. We are hesitant to believe what we cannot prove. We dismiss signs of God as coincidence even when we have stumbled right into holy.

What does it mean if God doesn't just whisper to those destined to be priests, nuns, or monks but to each and every one of us? What does it mean if God shows up everywhere, all the time, and we don't have to pray in a pew or go on a pilgrimage to feel the presence of God?

What if God is all around us—from soup kitchens in our cities to wooded trails in our national parks—as much as he is in the most sacred cathedrals? And what if we believed God is waiting and whispering, just like the dancing dots on our phones signaling an incoming message?

How would our lives be different if we believed God is present every day, as evidenced by the extraordinary stories of ordinary grace?

How often do we ask why God is not more present in our lives while dismissing the evidence when God shows up?

How would our world be different if we didn't just listen to whispers but acted upon them? We need to pay attention when we hear a whisper, no matter how inconvenient, unexpected, and uncomfortable it feels. We need to trust the whisper and *Do something about it*. But most importantly, we need to talk about what happens when we do listen. That is the only way to connect the God Dots and recognize the incredible weave between us all.

It's not coincidence. It's God.

There are burning bushes all around us, but we spend too much time extinguishing them and not enough time standing in awe of them.

Brazilian author Paulo Coelho, who wrote *The Alchemist*, told Oprah Winfrey in an interview:

> I think that courage is the first spiritual quality that you need to have. You don't need to have a good connection with God. You don't need to believe there is a God. But you need to have courage.[1]

It takes courage to listen to a whisper. It takes faith to step out of the life you know and into something completely unexpected.

When a whisper comes into our lives, and it feels like it is disrupting all our plans, it most certainly is. Usually, we recognize that first whisper at the moment when we are restless for purpose, wondering if this is the life we were really meant to live. It might happen when we are contemplating a job change or facing a health challenge.

At first, it might be just a whim of an idea that seems to have no relation to your present reality.

Become a teacher. But you have spent thirty years as an electrical engineer.

Write a book. But you don't believe you have anything to say.

Volunteer at a shelter. But you are fearful of who you might meet there.

Your fear voice will constantly try to drown out the quiet, small voice in your soul, but the funny thing about whispers is that they are incredibly persistent. Once you are finally ready to listen, the whisper will repeat so incessantly that you finally have no choice but to listen or pretend you never heard it.

Listening to a whisper will mean setting out on a new life path that will probably be a detour from the to-do voice you have been following your entire life. It will feel exactly as if you are headed into the woods. You can see a trail, but you have no idea where it leads. Whispers are like that. They take us to places we never expected and toward goals we never imagined for ourselves.

Trusting and listening to whispers are the way we begin to understand what we are meant to do in this world. It is the divine voice in our souls, reminding us why we came here. If you are a Christian, you will understand this as the Holy Spirit. If you are Jewish, you will call this divine force Ruach HaKodesh. If you have a different faith tradition or are not sure what you believe, you might just think of your whispers as what poet Cleo Wade calls *Heart Talk*.

However you define it, you have to be open to the idea in order to experience the current of grace running through this world.

Once you listen to a whisper and pay attention to the God Dots that follow, you will begin to make remarkable connections. It is that phenomenon of *nitzotzot*, that image of Indra's net—all of us igniting, shining, connecting to repair the world. If you have the courage to trust those whispers, you can experience a type of bravery you never thought possible.

I hope that after you read the stories in this book, you begin paying deep attention in *your* life to *your* whispers and connecting *your* God Dots. I know I am still learning and still trying to listen every day. The more I pay attention and the more I connect, the more I believe that I will never fully understand how this divine weave works—which is the point. To me, faith is all about believing even when there can be no certainty.

. . . .

Listening to your whispers will mean you have to risk being changed. Your to-do voice will argue that you are too busy to dream new dreams. Your fear voice will remind you that you are unqualified. Both voices will attempt to drown out the whisper that keeps beckoning you to the shore of a different life.

But maybe these God Dot stories have you asking some new questions.

Are you living the life you were meant to lead?

Are you wondering where God is in your life at the same time you are ignoring the signs that he is fully present?

Maybe you have already heard a whisper that feels inconvenient, unexpected, or uncomfortable. You might have dismissed it as a silly thought or an impossible dream because you felt unqualified. Yet at the same time, that whisper has been insistent. What should you do?

Trust the whisper.

Take the first next step and the next. Stay on the path to see where it might take you. There will never be a neon sign to follow, just small hints that you are going in the right direction. When you keep following those small signs and whispers, you will be able to look back and see how far you have come, while at the same time understanding how far you have to go.

You will begin connecting your own God Dots and believing you are part of a divine weave that ties you to other people's whispers. You will be led to a life you never thought possible. Even in moments when you feel lost, you will understand how you are holy found.

This new life—the one you were always meant to live—is found by listening.

It begins with a whisper.

Epilogue

MORE TO THE STORIES

While this book bears witness to many incredible and even seem-ingly impossible stories, it does not begin to explain the complexi-ties of the world in which we live. One thing is certain: the more I know, the more I understand that I don't know.

Albert Einstein is widely believed to have said, "There are two ways to live your life. One is as if everything is a miracle, and the other is to believe that nothing is." I choose to believe that every day is miraculous, and when we pay attention, the evidence is all around us.

The God Dot stories in this book are what convinced me that statement is true. Along the way there were other instances of grace in my life, but these stories were the ones that would not let me go. Once I examined them, I could not go back to a "maybe" faith. I had to have a "God is in the details" faith. I will never be certain or able to fully explain how all these complex connections can be true, but I am certain God is behind them.

While many of the extraordinary whispers led to creating some-thing big, like Bill and Betsy Blue starting HopeWay or Jackie Craig creating The Green Chair Project, several of these stories were about people who followed a whisper that did not involve building anything yet led to remarkable outcomes in the life of at least one person. Frances Hailey faithfully multiplied dollars and blessings. Dru Dougherty Abrams honored her son. Meg Robertson received and delivered a message from my father. Lucy Fields reunited with her twin, Ellie, and gave lifesaving help to Liz Clasen-Kelly and Lydia Reese. Bill Whelan followed a whisper that led to a LifeVest. Chris Locklear rewrote his life story of addiction and homelessness to help others. Julia and Jay Robinson began with praying for others, and their story continues to inspire on what it means to live life to the fullest. Livvi gave me faith in my writing in a way I will never forget.

. . . .

Here's what is happening today for those in this book who listened to and trusted the whisper to create something.

Betsy and Bill Blue (Charlotte, North Carolina). Their vision to create a world-class mental health treatment center became a reality, and it opened in 2016. Today **HopeWay** helps over eight hundred clients a year through residential and day treatment programs on a twenty-acre campus that includes walking trails, gardens, and, of course, a beautiful gymnasium with a plaque honoring Mitch Abrams. Since opening, HopeWay has helped more than four thousand people from thirty-nine states and four countries. It has recently expanded to include a veterans' program, an outpatient clinic, and an eating disorder program, and is beginning to serve adolescents. Since it opened, HopeWay has been led by the remarkable Dr. Alyson Kuroski-Mazzei, who keeps the vision alive through a dedicated team of over one hundred professionals. Learn more at HopeWay.org.

Caroline Bundy (Birmingham, Alabama). Her whisper to create the **Way Station** to serve Alabama youth became a reality. After four years spent raising over $4.2 million, Caroline and her team at AIDS Alabama held the grand opening on August 4, 2022. The Way Station is designed to serve the unique needs of homeless, runaway, and at-risk youth with an emergency overnight crisis stabilization shelter and a transitional living program for older youth. The Way Station also offers supportive services such as trauma-informed care and counseling; education through traditional schooling or GED; life, job, and housing skills; and love as youth navigate their way to successful adulthood. Caroline is now listening for her next whisper and believes it might have something to do with housing. Learn more about the Way Station at AidsAlabama.org/TheWayStation.

Liz Clasen-Kelly (Charlotte, North Carolina) followed a whisper in college to serve the homeless and has dedicated her life to that cause ever since. Today she is the executive director of **Roof Above**, which operates Moore Place and is the largest homeless service provider in North Carolina. Roof Above is an interfaith nonprofit and comprehensive homeless service provider, serving twelve hundred people per day through a spectrum of services ranging from street outreach and emergency shelter to permanent supportive housing. In 2022, Roof Above completed a $40 million capital campaign to add 150 additional permanent supportive housing units, rebuild a shelter, and create a community rental assistance fund. **Chris Locklear** remains the nursing manager for the scattered site program with Roof Above, helping formerly homeless people regain their lives and find hope. Learn more at RoofAbove.org.

Jackie Craig (Raleigh, North Carolina). What began in 2010 as a lamp, a toaster, and a church closet has become a thriving nonprofit, furnishing homes and changing lives. Today, **The Green Chair Project** has distributed over one hundred and fifty thousand furniture donations, provided over six thousand beds for children, and utilized over one hundred thousand volunteer hours. In 2018, when Hurricane Florence hit eastern North Carolina, Green Chair provided support for rebuilding from the devastating effects of the storm and collaborated with state agencies to serve over seven thousand households that experienced complete destruction. Jackie remained the executive director for thirteen years before retiring in 2023. She's listening for her next whisper and loving life as Nana to her two grandsons. Green Chair continues with a dedicated staff offering love, dignity, and hope every day to families who are finding their way home. Learn more at TheGreenChair.org.

Lesley Faulkner and Priscilla Chapman (Charlotte, North Carolina). Together with cofounder **Mary Beth Hollett**, Lesley and Priscilla launched **Furnish for Good** in 2019. In only five years, they have grown to be a thriving nonprofit that connects well-loved home furnishings to underserved communities through an experience of empowerment. Rather than simply donating items, Furnish for Good curates and showcases them so that recipients receive more than home furnishings—they receive self-respect and dignity. In 2022, they served over 576 people, including 328 adults and 248 children, through twenty-six local agencies. Since inception, they have coordinated over six hundred moves and delivered over thirteen thousand pieces of furniture, which not only helped families but kept those home furnishings out of landfills. In 2023, **Maggie Morton** became their first paid executive director. Maggie leads the dedicated staff and volunteers helping so many have a home of their own. Learn more at FurnishForGood.org.

Josephine "Miss Jo" Hutchison Morrison (Kingsport, Tennessee). The amazing Miss Jo, who began a new whisper at age 100, passed away at age 105 on April 9, 2022. In our last call together, Miss Jo said, "Stay open to opportunities, but do something that makes life easier or happier for people. Whether in your profession or your spare time, you are blessed in order to be a blessing." When she died, Miss Jo was well into accomplishing her goal of creating housing for those experiencing homelessness in Kingsport. When she was 103, she officially founded the **Kingsport Homeless Ministry** and began raising money for **Grace House**, a shelter and resource center. Over her lifetime, Miss Jo spent more than fifty years working on housing through Habitat for Humanity as well as being a longtime member of the Kingsport Affordable Housing Coalition. Her dying wish was to see Grace House open, and so she asked that for her 105th birthday, all gifts be made to the campaign. Miss Jo is remembered as a "shining light" in Kingsport. As of this writing, Grace House is still under development and accepting donations to make Miss Jo's dream a reality. Learn more at Kpthm.org.

Molly Painter (Raleigh, North Carolina). Inspired by women experiencing homelessness and the example of Moore Place, Molly Painter listened to her whisper to help build housing in Raleigh. Partnering with lead service provider CASA, NC, Molly successfully raised over $27 million for **King's Ridge**, which broke ground in 2022. Slated to open in 2024, King's Ridge will provide thirty apartments for families experiencing homelessness and seventy apartments for chronically homeless men and women. King's Ridge will be safe, permanent supportive housing, and it will reduce homelessness by 10 percent in Raleigh and Wake County. Learn more at CasaNC.org/KingsRidge/.

Caroline Hart (Crossnore, North Carolina). Caroline still works for Crossnore Communities, helping to raise as much as she can to transform the lives of children in North Carolina. Caroline, Jim, and McRae Hart officially became a family of seven in 2018 with the adoption of Cain, Aiden, Nevaeh, and Liam. Crossnore brings clinical expertise and compassionate care to children and families through four interconnected resource communities: therapy, family preservation, foster care and adoption, and youth independent living. Learn more at Crossnore.org.

· · · ·

Whether you are hearing a whisper to simply be kind and loving to one person or a whisper insistently calling you to a larger purpose, my advice is the same: *Trust the whisper.* Those whispers remind us why we came here and encourage us to not only do better but be better.

Lucille Clifton, an American poet, writer, and educator, wrote, "In the bigger scheme of things, the universe is not asking us to do something, the universe is asking us to be something. And that's a whole different thing."[1]

If you are hearing a whisper that there is something more you are meant to be or meant to do, or that something amazing in your life is more than a coincidence, then these stories are for you.

Let them be affirmation. Let them be signs you are on the right path. And even if you can't quite see what's ahead for you, let them light your way.

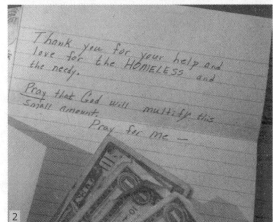

1. Moore Place. 2. A note from the Mailbox Angel. 3. Bill and Betsy Blue. 4. Mitch Abrams ready for a game.

5. Caroline Bundy opening the Way Station, Birmingham, Alabama (photo credit: Bham Now). 6. Miss Jo recording a video interview with Kathy. 7. Jackie Craig in The Green Chair Project. 8. Meg Roberston and Kathy.

9. Lucy and Ellie. 10. Lesley Faulkner (photo credit: Laura Meier). 11. Molly at the Women's Center in Raleigh. 12. Priscilla Chapman (photo credit: Lauren Belle Photography).

13. Liz Clasen-Kelly (photo credit: Rodney Scot Media Group). 14. "Papa CJ" and his family (photo credit: Holly Hennessee). 15. Bill Whelan. 16. Sloan, Jay, and Julia Robinson (photo credit: Knox Barker).

17. Team Raleigh at the King's Ridge groundbreaking (photo credit: Tyler Cunningham). 18. The complete Hart Family (photo credit: Mikaela Huff). 19. Andrea Dorsey Kirs.

Acknowledgments

Charlie: Thank you for believing in me and my whispers, and for all the early morning quiet for these pages to be written. It was a "love at first sight" whisper that led me to you, and I am so grateful for my goose.

Lauren, Pete, Anté, Charlie, Kailey, Maddie, Emma, and Connor: I am thankful beyond measure for all the girls, and now boys, in my life. I can't wait to see where your whispers lead you!

Louise and Allyson: Thank you always for the Green Girl sisterhood—I think Lindsay and Leighton are smiling and dancing.

Nancy Engen and Susan Izard: Thank you for always being willing to read early drafts and giving me very honest sisterly advice.

Blythe Daniels: Thank you for taking a chance on me and this book idea and working so hard to find it a good publishing home. Forever grateful to agents like you who give unknown writers like me a chance.

Patnacia Goodman: Thank you for bringing this book to Baker, and I will always be grateful you gave it a second look!

Lindsey Spoolstra, Rachel Freire O'Connor, Laura Powell, Brianna DeWitt, Eileen Hanson, Nadine Rewa, and the entire Baker Books team: Thank you for making this the best book it could be.

Deb Nichols: Thank you for being the first to read these words and, more importantly, giving me the encouragement that they might be good enough.

Carrie Banwell: Thank you for being an early reader and giving me sage advice. I will never forget our Chartres adventure and the moment you connected the perfect God Dot ending for this book.

Kristin Hills Bradberry: Thank you for reading and encouraging my writing. But especially thank you for all your wise counsel in years of Monday morning meetings that led to raising millions for HopeWay and Roof Above.

Julie Marr: Thank you for the title (*The Hundred Story Home*) that connected me to almost every God Dot in this book. And thanks to you and **Arkon Stewart** for beautifully convincing donors to support unlikely dreams like Moore Place and HopeWay.

Edwina Willis-Fleming: Thank you for handing me the courage card that read "Your book next" and believing it to be true. You never doubted even when I did.

Niki Hardy, Trina McNeilly, and Nicole Zasowski: Thank you for all your "mastermind" advice for this book and every other publishing whisper. I am grateful to my writer friends on this journey.

Kate Rademacher: Thank you for your encouragement and for being my author "phone a friend."

Liza Branch, Kathleen Richardson, and Julie Marr: Thank you for all the lunch laughter that always keeps Sister Mary Margaret grounded and real.

Caroline Simas: Thank you for all the creative inspiration and for the *first* celebration of this book contract.

Sally McMillan: You were an angel in my life with *The Hundred Story Home* and now are with the angels yourself. Still searching for blue butterflies and you.

• • • •

In some cases, I have changed names to honor confidentiality and health privacy concerns, but all these stories are true. Behind every story in this book are people who were part of the story yet were not named in the chapter, due to space constraints. Yet without that full cast of characters, it is likely the stories would not have happened the same way. I have tried to capture all of them here so that they remain a part of the collective whisper.

Chapter 1

Sarah Belk, Kim Belk, Angela Breeden, and Edwina Willis-Fleming: Thank you for being the force for good behind the first True Blessings. Without you believing in the first whisper to *Invite them to speak*, none of the rest of the stories would have ever happened. And, Sarah, you especially have been connected to more God Dots than I could ever name.

Paige James, Karen Pritchett, Anne Perper, and Paige Waugh: Thank you for all your help creating a first-time fundraising event, and thank you to all the table hosts who supported the very first True Blessings.

Chapter 2

Dale Mullennix: Thank you for giving this graphics girl a chance to reimagine my life and being brave enough to expand the mission of the Urban Ministry Center. You changed the way Charlotte treated those experiencing homelessness and, in doing so, changed the lives of thousands.

Joann Markley: Without you, Homeless to Homes never would have succeeded, and likely Moore Place would not exist. You serve everyone as if they were family and are far more than a case manager—you truly save lives.

Steve Barton, David Furman, Bill Holt, Jerry Licari, Hugh McColl, and Matt Wall: Thank you for being an incredible team that helped do the impossible in the worst of times. Moore Place would not exist without each of you and your dedication to seeing it built.

Caroline Chambre-Hammock: Thank you for being the exact right person at the exact right time to make Moore Place succeed. We could build a building, but you made it work and proved that everyone deserves a place to call home.

Chapters 3 and 4

There were literally hundreds of people who came alongside Betsy and Bill Blue to make the HopeWay dream a reality, but I especially want to recognize the other members of the founding board of HopeWay, including **Rob Buckfelder, Bob Dooley, Mike Elliott, Travis Hain, Margaret Jackson, David Neill, Steve Purdy, Jane Showalter, and Ann Stolz.**

Betsy and Bill Blue: Thank you for imagining for Charlotte what no one else could. Your whisper has changed the lives of thousands and will continue to transform mental health in our city, the state, and the region for years to come.

Bailey Patrick: Thank you for finding the miracle property that would become HopeWay and for your personal story of understanding how amethysts could one day become hope stones.

Morgan Liles: Thank you for being the very first employee of HopeWay and taking a leap of faith to believe in this dream with us.

Dr. Alyson Kuroski-Mazzei: Thank you for listening to your whisper to move from California to become the CEO and medical director of HopeWay. But more importantly, thanks for making HopeWay exactly what so many hoped and dreamed it might be.

And thank you to the incredible HopeWay medical support staff and team. You provide hope every day to hundreds of clients and families who need it.

Emily Hope Johnson: Thank you for stepping in at just the right moment and continuing to connect so many families to hope.

Dru Dougherty Abrams: Thank you for your courage in sharing your story and honoring your dear son, Mitch, through HopeWay.

Chapter 5

Beverly Burnett: Thank you for being the angel I needed ten thousand feet in the air. I hear your words every time I speak, and I am so grateful for my midair miracle.

Chapter 6

Rachel Estes: Thank you for believing in me as an author before I even believed in myself, and for bonding over bacon jam.

Melissa Leahey: Thank you for your wild and wonderful hopes for *The Hundred Story Home*. You made me believe too!

Caroline Bundy: Thank you for sharing your whisper and helping me understand what my next whisper could be. You have changed the lives of hundreds of teens who will probably never know how complicated that simple solution was to build.

Chapter 7

Meg Robertson and Liz Clasen-Kelly: I am thankful for the miracle that brought us all together, and I can't wait to see what big magic awaits ahead.

Chapter 9

Martha Crampton: Thank you for an invitation to speak to a book club that turned out to be the beginning of so much more! You were the God Dot connecting me to Jackie, and I remain grateful.

Jackie Craig: I am so glad I can't read emails and ended up on the wrong/right doorstep. I am grateful for all the God Dot connections we share, even the tough ones.

Beth Smoot: Thank you for being the perfect partner for Jackie to begin creating The Green Chair Project and all its many ripple effects.

Graham Satisky, Rae Marie Czuhai, and Astra Barnes: I am grateful our God Dots are connected through Green Chair and for all you do to help bring people home with dignity.

Chapters 10 and 11

Mary Beth Hollett: Thank you for insisting I attend that writing conference, because that was the beginning of everything I could not imagine for myself. And I am so glad **Lesley and Priscilla** became "chiefs" with you. You three are amazing!

Laurie Martin: Thank you for all your early encouragement to create a furniture program in Charlotte and for the many you have helped in the community with Simplicity Serves.

Maggie Morton: Thank you for taking that leap of faith to lead Furnish for Good—I can't wait to see how it grows under your guidance.

Chapter 12

Lucy Fields and Ellie: Thank you for being the best example of sisterly love and of how everyone deserves a home. You know who you are and how special your bond will always be.

Chapter 13

Team Raleigh—Molly Painter, Katie Koon, Betty Nelson, and Sally Tanner: Thank you for never wavering in your belief that you could and should do more. You have changed what Raleigh thought was possible, and now hundreds of lives will be changed.

Chapter 15

You don't get through a medical crisis without extraordinary doctors, family, and friends. Charlie and I are lucky to have an abundance of each, but in this chapter our gratitude is especially for the following:

Dr. Omar Ali: Thank you for saving the one life most dear to me.

Rick Packer, CEO of Zoll Medical Corporation: Thank you for answering Bill's call and for the LifeVest that gave us a way to finally go home.

To learn more about SCAD (Spontaneous Coronary Artery Dissection), visit ScadAlliance.org.

Chapter 16

Chris Locklear: Thank you for persevering even when you thought you were giving in. God did have a better plan—first with HopeWay and then Roof Above.

Chapter 17

Julia Robinson: Thank you for your heart for the homeless, which sealed both our friendship and now all the God Dots that continue to connect us—including the Camino to come!

Lou and Buzz O'Brien: Thank you for your encouragement, kind words, and wonderful daughter.

Ken Keeton: Thank you for starting the Prayers in the Park ministry at Holy Trinity Episcopal Church in Greensboro, North Carolina, and for your compassion to do more.

Louise Brady and Jean Anne Ferner: Thank you for being the dearest friends to Julia and Jay, traveling the many miles so often to support them in Colorado.

Chapters 18 and 19

Thank you to the ministries and dedicated staff of **Healing Transitions, Bloom Here, and The Women's Center in Raleigh** for supporting Ellie on her journey and also so many other women experiencing homelessness.

Chapter 20

Caroline and Jim Hart: Thank you for an incredible example of love and for opening your hearts and home to create a family of seven.

   Brett Loftis and the entire Crossnore staff: Thank you for the incredible work you do that saves the lives of children like Cain, Aiden, Nevaeh, and Liam every day.

Chapter 21

Livvi: Thank you for listening to the whispers to pick up the book and write me—I hope you are finally home.

Chapter 22

Beth McCombs Gast: Thank you for being my fifty-year friend. While I miss our third amigo, I am so grateful to still have you in the world.

   Tina Mohr: Thank you for sharing the amazing Andrea with me and allowing me to be a part of her last day. I believe in our divine connection and that Andrea made certain we would stay friends.

Discussion Guide

Dear Reader,

Thank you for taking the time to read Trust the Whisper. *I hope it will help you recognize your own whispers. I also hope that by writing these stories and providing this study guide for deeper reflection, I've given you tools that can help you begin to answer your own quiet callings.*

I don't know what's around the corner for you or me, but I have learned three things. One, there is no final destination in life. As soon as I think one road has ended, it turns and invites me toward a new horizon. Two, I believe the unexpected waits for each of us, and that unplanned path is intricately woven with others whom we are yet to meet. Three, finding that path begins with a whisper and believing there is something to hear.

So keep listening and let me know, **what's your whisper?**

Kathy

Chapter 1 *Denver: The First Whisper*

1. Can you relate to the idea of a to-do voice and a fear voice? How have they helped you? How have they limited you?

2. Denver helped Kathy see homelessness in a way she could never "unsee." Have you volunteered at a similar soup kitchen or shelter? How did it change your perceptions about hunger, homelessness, or affordable housing?

3. Kathy wrote that she believes there is something each of us is meant to do in this world. How do you see your purpose, and how might it relate to others?

Chapter 2 *Frances: The Next God Dot*

1. At the beginning of this chapter, Kathy introduces the idea of Housing First. Have you ever heard of this concept, and is there a similar program in your community?

2. Frances Hailey faithfully donated her $10, hoping it might "bless and multiply." Have you ever helped a similar campaign? Why did you give, and what were the results?

3. In this chapter, Kathy writes about noticing "the holy all around us." How have you noticed the holy around you?

Chapter 3 *Betsy: A Grace Walk*

1. Betsy and Bill Blue were frustrated by the lack of mental health care. Do you know someone with a similar mental health challenge? How has that affected them or you?

2. When Betsy found the letter in Maine, she felt it was the exact sign she needed. Have you ever asked for a sign, and did you receive it?

3. Betsy said that God "puts people in our lives to be the hands and feet we need." Do you agree? How have you experienced that in your life?

Chapter 4 *Dru: Remembering Mitch*

1. Mitch would at times be homeless even though he could have stayed housed with his parents. Did understanding that Mitch came from a family of means change any views you had about homelessness?

2. Mitch ended up taking his own life before HopeWay was finished. Have you experienced the loss of a friend or family member through suicide? What hopes might you have had for them?

3. At the grand opening, Betsy recalls not feeling lonely anymore. Have you had a similar experience of finding a community of people who shared a problem, and that connection helped you?

Chapter 5 *Beverly: Airplane Angel*

1. In reading Bruce Wilkinson's book, Kathy learns about his premise of missing everyday miracles. Do you agree? What "everyday miracles" have you witnessed?

2. Becoming an Al-Anon speaker was not something Beverly planned. Have you or someone you know ended up on a very different life path? What was the turning point?

3. Kathy writes, "I had almost let my miracle go unnoticed and unrevealed." Do you have your own story of when you might have missed a miracle?

Chapter 6 *Caroline: The Simple Solution*

1. Kathy's book ended up with Rachel Estes, who felt it was a "chill bump connection." What do you think she meant by that? Have you ever had a similar feeling?

2. Caroline Bundy said that even as a child, the problem of homelessness bothered her. Do you have an early memory

of a social problem that bothered you? What have you done about it?

3. Caroline said about the Way Station, "If I had known what it was going to grow to be, I am not sure I would have done it." Have you ever had an idea but stopped because of fear or because it felt too overwhelming? Is it still something you would like to consider?

Chapter 7 *Meg: The Tai Chi Studio Windowsill*

1. Meg was drawn to service at an early age. Do you have a heart for service that goes back to when you were a child? Do you remember what it was, or who influenced you?

2. Kathy wished her father had known about her present life. Have you lost someone, and what would you want them to know about your present life?

3. The messages Meg receives and the idea of "thin places" have helped her become less afraid of death. What are your beliefs about death, and how have you come to that belief?

Chapter 8 *Miss Jo: Never Too Late*

1. Miss Jo did not consider her age as a barrier to starting a new project. What were your thoughts about Miss Jo starting her project at age one hundred?

2. Miss Jo experienced resistance about building that is called NIMBYism, meaning "not in my backyard." Does your community have similar fights on housing and where to build?

3. Kathy writes about people who feel they have "missed their chance" to do something because they believe they

are "too old." Do you have that worry, and did this chapter change your views about what might be possible?

Chapter 9 *Jackie: A Lamp and a Toaster*

1. Kathy writes that "listening and paying attention are the key" for God Dot connections. How have you seen that to be true so far in the book? How have you experienced that in your life?
2. Jackie was struck by the "What Are You Waiting For?" exhibit she helped install. Have you experienced a sense of waiting in your life?
3. Understanding how experiences in her life came together to prepare her for Green Chair, Jackie said, "God uses everything we do." How might this be true in your life?

Chapter 10 *Lesley: "Yellow Pants" Whisper*

1. Kathy writes about many divine appointments in her life. Have you had a divine appointment in your life?
2. This chapter also introduces the idea of *nitzotzot*, "divine sparks," and the concept of *tikkun olam*. Do these ideas correspond with your own beliefs, or do you have different views?
3. Lesley's whisper felt "too big" to listen to at the time. Have you ever had a desire to help with something that felt too overwhelming? How could you break it down to one simple first step?

Chapter 11 *Priscilla: The Next Forty Years*

1. Priscilla Chapman said she was searching for a "forty-year thing." What's your forty-year thing?

2. Priscilla's family was known as a "successful" family, yet her brother was actually struggling with addiction. Have you experienced this in your life? Are there situations you kept secret? What would happen if you sought help?

3. Lesley said the experience of working on Furnish for Good changed her perception of gentrification. Is there a social justice issue you have come to see from a different point of view?

Chapter 12 *Lucy: The Lost Twin*

1. Kathy met Lucy Fields as she was hearing a whisper to find Ellie. Have you ever lost touch with someone important in your life? What would it mean to reconnect?

2. Lucy felt stretched between her son's physical illness and her sister's mental illness. Have you faced similar demands, and how did you find ways to cope?

3. Lucy talks about making "bold choices one step at a time" to shift our circumstances. Do you agree? How have you found this to be true or untrue in your life?

Chapter 13 *Molly: The One*

1. This chapter begins by talking about people who listened to their whisper. "For 'the one,' the whisper wasn't a should. It was a *must*." Have you ever felt that way about something? What was it, and what did you do?

2. When she began volunteering at the women's center, Molly Painter found much more was needed. Have you had a similar experience? What did you believe was needed, and what did you discover?

3. It turned out that Ellie, Lucy, and Molly were all connected, and it was a "BIG WOW" for Molly. Have you ever had a BIG WOW kind of God moment? What happened?

Chapter 14 *Liz: Saving Isaac*

1. Liz said that it was "truly sacred" to meet Lucy the way she did. Have you ever been the person someone needed in a crisis, or has someone been that for you? Did you find it easier to give help or to receive it?

2. Liz said the first question she would ask God would be about healing. What is the first question you would want to ask God?

3. At the end of the chapter, Liz said, "We are all vessels. We all get invited into this larger story if we choose to listen." Have you ever felt you were a vessel invited into a larger story?

Chapter 15 *Bill: The LifeVest*

1. Bill Whelan woke up wondering if Charlie needed anything. Have you ever had a similar experience of someone showing up with exactly what you needed, when you needed it?

2. Bill said, "I think God was right there with me, nudging me and guiding me." Have you ever felt God nudging and guiding you?

3. The quote from Francis Collins about science and faith is that we need to "embrace both realms." Do you believe this to be true? How do you balance faith and science in your life?

Chapter 16 *Chris: God's Better Plan*

1. Chris Locklear was raised with "morals at an early age." How did your upbringing create either a strong or an unstable foundation in your life?

2. For years, Chris and his family felt hopeless about his situation. Have you or someone you loved ever battled addiction? How did you find hope?

3. Chris said at one point he begged God to take him out of this world. Have you ever prayed for something and received a better answer?

Chapter 17 *Julia: Prayers in the Park*

1. Julia Robinson and her husband found out that "Prayers aren't enough." How have you put your faith into action on an issue?

2. Julia had to tell her soulmate, "It's okay to go." Have you ever been with a friend or family member at the end of life? How has that experience affected how you view your own mortality?

3. Julia wanted to create meaning with the seventy-seven-day "Live Like Jay" tribute. How would you want friends to honor your life based on the values you hold dear?

Chapter 18 *Molly, Lucy, Ellie, and Jackie: Room for All*

1. When her brother died, Molly asked herself, "What am I really doing with my life?" Have you asked yourself this question? What did it help you discover?

2. Ellie said, "Even birds have nests, and animals have a den, but if you don't have that as a human, you will never feel

safe." Did her statement make you consider the problem of homelessness differently?

3. Ellie shared that she would look in the mirror and ask herself, "How did you become this?" Have you ever realized your life had become something you never intended? What happened, and what steps did you take after that?

Chapter 19 *Lydia, Lucy, and Ellie: An Angel Donation*

1. Several of the stories in this book have now interconnected, with people who were once strangers becoming integral parts of each other's stories. Has this ever happened to you? How do you explain those connections?

2. Lydia describes Lucy Fields as "a beautiful resource in my life." Who are the beautiful resources in your life, and have you ever told them so? How might you show your gratitude?

3. This chapter also reveals the connection between Lucy, Ellie, Lydia, and Linda. Kathy writes it was "beyond coincidence or serendipity." Do you agree? How do you see God in this story?

Chapter 20 *Caroline: Mountain People*

1. Caroline and Jim lost two pregnancies and were never able to get pregnant again. Have you or a friend suffered a miscarriage or infertility? What has that experience been like?

2. Caroline wanted to quit because the stories of the children were so difficult, but Brett convinced her otherwise. Have you ever been overwhelmed in trying to help solve a problem? What advice helped you?

3. Caroline and Jim came to believe their whisper was to adopt four children and create a family of seven. Do you think you would have listened to a whisper like that? Do you know any similar stories?

Chapter 21 *Livvi: Longing for Home*

1. Kathy writes that her whisper to *Write it down* turned out to be the connection to most of the stories in this book. Do you think she had that whisper in order to know these people and write their stories?

2. Livvi describes "traveling around the country mostly on foot since I was eighteen." How do you think this ties to the problems Caroline Bundy described in chapter 6, which led to the Way Station?

3. Kathy writes that her favorite line was Livvi's admission about struggling with "the whole God thing." Do you struggle with that? Have you ever seen doors open in your life?

Chapter 22 *Andrea: The Last Connection*

1. Kathy writes that she, Andrea, and Beth were friends for over fifty years. What are some of your longest friendships, and how do you stay connected?

2. Kathy and Tina are with Andrea during her end-of-life care. Have you ever been with someone in their last hours, and did it change how you would want your end-of-life care to be handled?

3. Tina was asking for a sign from her sister at the same time Kathy was "answering" Andrea. How do you explain this timing and connection?

Chapter 23 A *Divine Weave*

1. Which stories or which people in this book have made the most impact on you?
2. Has reading these stories of people listening to their whispers made you reconsider what might be a coincidence and what might be a divine connection?
3. What do you believe might be whispering to you? Are you ready to listen?

Notes

Chapter 1 Denver

1. Kathy writes the full story of her meeting with Denver Moore and all that happened as a result in her first memoir, *The Hundred Story Home: A Memoir about Finding Faith in Ourselves and Something Bigger* (repr. Nashville: Nelson, 2018).

Chapter 2 Frances

1. Frederick Buechner, *Secrets in the Dark: A Life in Sermons* (New York: Harper One, 2006), 183.

Chapter 5 Beverly

1. Bruce Wilkinson, *You Were Born for This: Seven Keys to a Life of Predictable Miracles* (Colorado Springs: Multnomah, 2009), 3.

Chapter 7 Meg

1. Jocelyn A. Sideco, "We Celebrate 'Thin Places' Where Meeting Occurs," *National Catholic Review*, October 31, 2019, https://www.ncronline.org/opinion/young-voices/we-celebrate-thin-places-where-meeting-occurs.

Chapter 10 Lesley

1. Kathleen Tessaro, *Rare Objects* (New York: Harper, 2016), 200.
2. "Tikkun Olam: Why We Were Born into a Broken World and What We Are to Do about It," Chabad.org, accessed September 20, 2023, https://www.chabad.org/library/article_cdo/aid/3591946/jewish/Tikkun-Olam.htm.

Chapter 11 Priscilla

1. Project I Am, accessed September 20, 2023, https://officialprojectiam.com.

Chapter 12 Lucy

1. Rosario Trifiletti, "Frequently Asked Questions," PANDAS/PANS Institute, accessed September 20, 2023, https://www.pandaspansinstitute.com/faqs.

Chapter 15 Bill

1. Francis S. Collins, *The Language of God: A Scientist Presents Evidence for Belief* (New York: Simon & Schuster, 2006), 6.

Chapter 22 Andrea

1. Unitarian Universalist Association, "Indra's Magnificent Jeweled Net," Building Bridges Workshop Curriculum, accessed September 20, 2023, https://www.uua.org/re/tapestry/youth/bridges/workshop7/indra.

Chapter 23 A Divine Weave

1. Oprah Winfrey, "Paulo Coelho, Part 2: Your Journey of Self-Discovery," *The Best of Oprah's Super Soul* (podcast), August 10, 2017, https://www.oprah.com/own-podcasts/paulo-coelho-part-2-your-journey-of-self-discovery-from-august-10-2017.

Epilogue

1. Grateful Living, "Lucille Clifton," Word for the Day, accessed September 20, 2023, https://grateful.org/word-for-the-day/in-the-bigger-scheme-of-things-the-universe-is-not-asking-us-to-do-something-the-universe-is-asking-us-to-be-something-and-thats-a-whole-different-thing/.

KATHY IZARD is an award-winning author and an advocate for housing and mental health services in Charlotte, North Carolina. She co-led the citywide effort to build Moore Place, Charlotte's first permanent supportive housing for chronically homeless men and women, and was instrumental in the development of HopeWay, Charlotte's first residential mental health treatment center. She wrote about her efforts in her memoir *The Hundred Story Home*, which received a 2017 Christopher Award for inspirational nonfiction. Kathy is a national speaker and retreat leader encouraging women to be changemakers in their communities.

Both a mom and a grandmother, Kathy did not start writing and publishing until after she was fifty years old. She believes it is never too late to follow a dream or trust a whisper.

WANT TO LEARN MORE ABOUT THE AUTHOR?
Learn about all Kathy's books and speaking at www.KathyIzard.com
Learn about workshops and retreats with Kathy at www.WomenFaith Story.com

DO YOU HAVE A WHISPER?
Kathy writes on Substack about people who have listened to their whispers. Read more stories at WhatsYourWhisper.substack.com

WHAT'S YOUR WHISPER?
If you want to be featured, tell Kathy your story at WomenFaithStory @gmail.com

 @Kathyizardclt and @womenfaithstory